I0811066

PRAISE FOR

HEAVEN AND HELL

"For too long, eschatology has been treated as if it's only about colossal events around the globe in the end times. But personal eschatology affects everyone, for all people die and ask the question, "What will happen to me?" Kevin Zuber cuts through the confusion and takes you back to the biblical basis for your beliefs about life and death. Instead of relying on sentimental feelings and vague speculations about heaven and hell, this book provides a straightforward view into what God has to say about life's most ultimate questions."

— Dr. Bryan Litfin
Professor of Bible & Theology
Liberty University, Rawlings School of Divinity, Lynchburg, VA

Most people wonder about what happens when we die. Clearly this is one of the most important issues addressed by the Bible. Nevertheless, it is sometimes hard to determine just exactly what the Scriptures say about it. That's why Kevin Zuber's book is so significant. Combining the skills of a Bible scholar, a systematic theologian and a caring pastor, Dr. Zuber lays out a biblical understanding of what lies beyond the grave. In clear and compelling language, this book brings light to the most avoided but most crucial subject for every person.

—Michael Rydelnik
Interim Vice President and Academic Dean
Professor of Jewish Studies, Moody Bible Institute
Host/Bible Teacher, Moody Radio's
Open Line with Dr. Michael Rydelnik

Titles in the Institute for the Christian Life Series

Published in 2023

Heaven and Hell: A Survey of the Biblical Doctrines of Personal Eschatology (Kevin Zuber)

The Forgotten Attributes of God: God's Nature and Why It Matters (Peter Sammons)

Old Testament Survey 1: Genesis to Esther (Nathan LeMaster)

Well Done: A Strategy for Life Stewardship (Reagan Rose)

Becoming a Worthy Reader: How to Read and Study the Bible (Kevin Zuber)

Coming in 2024 (tentative titles)

New Testament Survey 1 (Mark Zhakevich)

The Art of Biblical Discernment (Phil Johnson)

Biblical Gender and Sexuality (Mike Riccardi)

The Ordinary Church (John MacArthur)

Spiritual Gifts (Nate Busenitz)

Coming in 2025 (tentative titles)

Prayer (Carl Hargrove)

Old Testament Survey 2 (Nathan LeMaster)

Sanctification (Mike Riccardi)

Church Leadership (Kevin Zuber)

Offices of Christ (Peter Sammons)

Coming in 2026 (tentative titles)

Apologetics (Kevin Zuber)

Discipleship and Counseling (author TBD)

The Gospel of Grace (Peter Sammons)

The Trinity (Peter Sammons and Mike Riccardi)

New Testament Survey 2 (Mark Zhakevich)

SOUND DOCTRINE

Heaven and Hell

A Survey of the Biblical Doctrines of Personal Eschatology

KEVIN D. ZUBER

CLC PUBLICATIONS
Fort Washington, PA 19034

Heaven and Hell: A Survey of the Biblical Doctrines of Personal Eschatology
The Institute for the Christian Life Series

Published by CLC Publications

USA: P.O. Box 1449, Fort Washington, PA 19034
www.clcpublications.com

UK: Kingsway CLC Trust
Unit 5, Glendale Avenue, Sandycroft, Flintshire, CH5 2QP
www.equippingthechurch.com

ISBN (paperback): 978-1-61958-364-1
ISBN (ebook): 978-1-61958-378-8

Printed in the United States of America

Italics in Scripture quotations are the emphasis of the author.

For Diane

CONTENTS

Series Foreword

The Institute for the Christian Life Series

From the time the Lord called me to Grace Community Church, I have had two primary goals: to preach the Word of God faithfully (2 Tim. 4:2) and to entrust the truth to faithful men (2:2). In keeping with those priorities, The Master's Seminary has played a key role in training future pastors to handle the Word accurately and defend its truth boldly. These Master's men have gone out to serve and shepherd churches across the nation and around the world.

Several years ago, to assist these faithful pastors in their shepherding work, the seminary created a lay-training program, comprised of online video courses. The Institute for the Christian Life (originally called the Institute for Church Leadership) is designed to train lay people in four fundamental categories: Bible Knowledge, Sound Doctrine, Christian Living, and Shepherding Care.

The ICL is designed to bring biblical training, theological instruction, and practical ministry into the pew and the living room—making these indispensable tools accessible to believers at all levels of spiritual maturity and church leadership. This book series complements those online courses, as an aid for small group discussion and individual study.

My prayer for you as you read this book, and engage with its content through the ICL, is that you would grow in the grace and knowledge of the Lord Jesus Christ. As the apostle Paul expressed in Ephesians 1:18–19, "I pray that the eyes of your heart may be enlightened, so that you will know what is the hope of His calling, what are the riches of the glory of His inheritance in the saints, and what is the surpassing greatness of His power toward us who believe."

John MacArthur
Pastor, Grace Community Church, Sun Valley, California
Chancellor, The Master's University and Seminary

Editorial Preface

Dr. KEVIN ZUBER (PhD, Trinity Evangelical Divinity School) serves as the Chair of the Theology Department at The Master's Seminary. With over 25 years of pastoral experience and 20 years in training students in higher education, he is uniquely gifted to help believers with their personal eschatology. The most important questions, posed by children and philosophers alike, center around what happens after death. We all need to be able to answer the vital questions related to the end of all things.

Charles Spurgeon once said, "Some of us know what it is to lie for days and weeks, looking into eternity, until our eyes have been able to gaze steadily on death and all the future, and we have grown so used to the prospect, and so peaceful in reference to it, that we have almost been sorry to come back again to life and its trials and sins."

What is so profound and convicting about this thought is that it reminds us how infrequently we consider vital doctrines such as Heaven and Hell, and how those truths impact the way we live our daily lives. In this book, Dr. Zuber provides a primer to eschatology by equipping the believer with an understanding of what happens upon death. It introduces the student to the worldview and hermeneutics involved in surveying both the Old Testament and New Testament to formulate a comprehensive eschatology. This study touches on the rapture, the tribulation period, the question of purgatory, the resurrections, the eschatological judgments, the eternal state, and personal destiny, among other aspects, so that the student of Scripture will be equipped to better understand God's word.

P. Sammons

Peter Sammons, PhD
Faculty Associate in Systematic Theology
The Master's Seminary

Introduction

When my mother was in her early eighties, she found herself a widow, in declining health and with diminishing mental capacities, living not in her own home with her family, but alone in an assisted living facility. Hers was not a particularly unusual story; in fact, most of the other residents in her wing of the "home for the aged" were in very similar circumstances. She was not particularly happy about being at this stage of life, but she was mostly content and, in a way, the years she spent in this setting were bittersweet for our relationship.

Because my siblings lived farther away than I did and because I had already become her legal representative, it fell to me to be the one to provide most directly for her needs. About once or twice a month (and when circumstances permitted or required, more often than that) I would make the three-hour drive from Indiana to Iowa to spend two or three days with her. We developed a something of a routine on these visits. We would eat at one of her favorite restaurants. We would take long drives through old neighborhoods and places where happy memories were revived. We went to the shopping mall, the zoo, the farmers market, and to more restaurants. After each adventure we would spend the evening in her apartment, watching reruns of her favorite television shows. And we would reminisce. And (somewhat to my surprise) we had some serious conversations about life and death. These conversations often led her to ask me questions.

Some of her questions were: *What is death? What is death like? What will it be like when I die? What will happen to me after I die? Will I be happy after I die? Will I know I have lived and died? Are you going to die?* (I think she was concerned that I would die before her.) When she started asking such questions, at first I sometimes tried to change the subject; but she rebuked me and said, "You are a pastor—you should know these things."

I somewhat reluctantly realized I needed to engage her questions more directly and forthrightly. I began to understand that she was not looking for platitudes (and actually, she seemed more lucid during these brief conversations than she was most of the rest of the time). I came to understand that in her circumstances (*especially* in her circumstances!) and at her stage in life, these were not idle, disinterested, or merely philosophical queries. Nor were they morbid, gloomy, or disconsolate questions. My mother was a Christian, a believer; her hope in Jesus Christ may not have been deep, but it was secure. Still, she had questions. I wish I had written this book before she went "to be at home with the Lord" (2 Cor. 5:8).

This book is about more than the title alone indicates; it will certainly have much to say about heaven and hell, but it will deal with a number of other issues and answer a number of other questions that most of mankind has asked about death and the life thereafter. Technically, this is a book about *personal eschatology.*

Personal Eschatology

The subject of "eschatology" is the study of "last things" or "end times"; from the Greek *eschtos*, "last," and *logos*, "word; study of."[1] The wider subject of general (Biblical) eschatology is most often concerned with end-time events, such as the rapture of the church,[2] the future of national Israel, the tribulation, the millennial kingdom, the new heavens and new earth.[3]

Personal eschatology is mostly focused on the matter of death and the afterlife. It deals with questions about the experience of death and the future state of individuals—be it the intermediate state (immediately after death but before judgment) or the permanent state (i.e., heaven, hell, or some other eternal state) of individual persons. Of course, the subjects of general and personal eschatology intersect at a number of points; however, in this book the focus will be on the personal aspects of eschatology; matters more pertinent to general eschatology, while not ignored, will not be dealt with in depth.

---

1 See William D. Mounce, ed., *Mounce's Complete Expository Dictionary of Old and New Testament Words* (Grand Rapids, MI: Zondervan, 2006) s.v. "Last," 391–92.

2 See John Hart, ed., *The Evidence for the Rapture: A Biblical Case for Pretribulationism* (Chicago, IL: Moody Publishers, 2015); John F. Walvoord, *The Rapture Question* (Grand Rapids, MI: Zondervan: 2010).

3 See Leon Wood, *The Bible and Future Events* (Grand Rapids, MI: Zondervan, 1973) and Paul Benware, *Understanding End Times Prophecy: A Comprehensive Approach* (Chicago: Moody Publishers, revised edition 2006). These books will provide the reader with a good, biblically informed overview of the full doctrines of eschatology that are assumed in this book. See also Appendix B.

An Unpleasant Subject

Death is not a happy subject, to say the least. It is, in fact, a most unpleasant one, for most people. Generally speaking, those who live in Western cultures avoid talking about death except in the abstract. The fact of death is often masked in euphemisms ("he expired," "she passed away"); the process of dying is often segregated to clinical settings (hospitals and hospice centers); the deceased are processed in funeral homes (a location that is never used for any function other than services for the deceased). About the only times people think even semi-seriously about death is when someone close to them dies, when a loved one is elderly or terminally ill, or when they buy life insurance (another euphemism—it is actually death insurance). For many people, death is something of an abstract reality; they know it's a possibility (actually, of course, it's an inevitability!), but unless it happens to someone close to them, death is relatively remote. It is addressed as if it were merely hypothetical, such as when a life insurance agent tells a potential customer, "You need this insurance in case you die."

On the other hand, in a macabre irony, depictions of death occur prominently in popular entertainment, such as movies and television shows. (One of my mother's favorite shows was "Murder, She Wrote"—the viewers could expect to witness at least one death in every episode.) But these fictional deaths are known by the viewer to be just that—fictional. Only the minor characters die, and even if a well-known actor is killed in one movie or episode, everyone knows he or she will be seen in the next movie or episode—as a different character in a new role. In any case, once again, in such ways death is abstracted from the everyday world.

Inevitable

At times, however, death is not an abstract reality. For such times, there are secular and semi-academic resources that address the reality and process of death,[4] and hospice services that offer guidance on dealing, in a practical way, with the issues of death and dying.[5] These resources can be helpful,

4 One such resource is Elizabeth Kubler-Ross, *On Death and Dying: What the Dying Have to Teach Doctors, Nurses, Clergy and Their Own Families* (New York: Scribner, fiftieth anniversary edition 2011).

5 See, for instance, Mayo Clinic Staff, "Hospice care: Comforting the terminally ill," Mayo Clinic, https://www.mayoclinic.org/healthy-lifestyle/end-of-life/in-depth/hospice-care/art-20048050. Accessed June 29, 2022.

but they ultimately do not address the questions that remain after a loved one dies; nor do they answer the very existential question—"What will happen to me after I die?" This was Hamlet's puzzle: "But that the dread of something after death, / The undiscovered country from whose bourn, / No traveler returns, puzzles the will."[6]

As self-conscious beings, we know that we will die. Beyond that, the only source that can answer the question, "What will happen to me after I die?" and resolve Hamlet's puzzle, is the Bible. This book will explore the Bible's doctrine on the reality of death for every human being, the destiny after death for those who believe in the saving work of Jesus Christ, and the very different destiny for those who do not.

Study Questions:

1. What is eschatology?
2. How does personal eschatology differ from general eschatology?
3. Why do many people avoid the subject of personal eschatology?
4. How do some people avoid the subject of death?
5. Why should believers study the subject of personal eschatology?

6 William Shakespeare, *Hamlet*, Act III, Scene 1.

1

Death and All Humanity

The first thing, then, is to inquire what death, which seems to be so well understood, really is; for some imagine death to be the departure of the soul from the body; others think that there is no such departure, but that soul and body perish together, and that, the soul is extinguished with the body. Of those who think that the soul does depart from the body, some believe in its immediate dissolution; others fancy that it continues to exist for a time; and others believe that it lasts forever.

Marcus Tullius Cicero (106 BC–43 BC)
Tusculan Disputations, Book 1

The Fact of Death

THE FIFTH CHAPTER OF the book of Genesis is something of a surprise to many students and readers of the Bible. It is a list of names; one or two are familiar (Adam, perhaps Seth, and maybe Methuselah), but most are entirely unheard of. It is a list of men—fathers and sons—who lived incredibly long lives (the longest was Methuselah—969 years!). The list is in a formulaic pattern: first, the father's age at the birth of the son; then, the son's birth; a note about the births of other sons and daughters (not named); and finally, the total number of years the father lived. And then, at the end of each entry, a simple, emphatic notation: "and he died" (Hebrew, *wayyāmōṯ*). This addendum occurs eight times: Adam (Gen. 5:5), Seth (5:8), Enosh (5:11), Kenan (5:14), Mahalalel (5:17), Jared (5:20), Methuselah (5:27), and Lamech (5:31), the father of Noah. (The exception to this pattern in the text is Enoch, the man who "walked with God." He alone was not among those who died; instead, the text records that "God took him," 5:24.) This repetition of "and he died" is for emphasis—the whole chapter "stresses that death had invaded the human family."[1]

1 Allen P. Ross, *Creation and Blessing: A Guide to the Study and Exposition of Genesis* (Grand Rapids, MI: Baker Academic, 1996), 176.

The same point can be made by a survey of the history of the kings of Israel and Judah as recorded in First Kings, Second Kings, and Second Chronicles. The accounts of the kings (good and bad) typically (and naturally) end with a note such as "he slept with his fathers" (1 Kings 2:10 of David; 11:43 of Solomon; 14:31 of Rehoboam; 15:8 of Abijam; 15:24 of Asa; 16:6 of Baasha; 16:28 of Omri; 22:40 of Ahab; 2 Kings 10:35 of Jehu; 13:13 of Joash; 14:16 of Jehoash; 14:29 of Jeroboam; 15:7 of Azariah; 15:22 of Menahem; 15:38 of Jotham; 16:20 of Ahaz; 20:21 of Hezekiah; 21:18 of Manasseh) or simply a notation acknowledging the act of their deaths. Thus even in the geo-political story line of "the nation (of Israel) among the nations," the reality and inevitability of death comes somberly into view.

It is a stark reminder of the events of Genesis 3.

The Cause of Death: "Sin means Death"

In Genesis 3 is recorded the first sin of human beings, what theologians call "the fall" of the human race, and the "original sin of Adam." God had placed man (Adam and Eve) in the Garden of Eden (Gen. 2:8) and He had given the man an abundance from which to eat and sustain himself (2:16). This was to demonstrate God's abundant goodness, provision, and grace. There was only one restriction: "from the tree of the knowledge of good and evil you shall not eat" (2:17). This was meant to test Adam's obedience to the Lord God. The penalty for disobedience could not have been clearer, "for in the day you eat from it you will surely die" (2:17). This principle—"sin" against the absolutely holy God means death—was established from the earliest days of man's existence on this planet. This principle was reiterated in every Old Testament sacrifice (Lev. 1–8, 16). The principle was reiterated succinctly by the apostle Paul in Romans 6:23: "the wages of sin is death." Paul is simply affirming, "Sinners get what they have earned. Death is no arbitrary sentence, but the inevitable consequence of their sin."[2]

That principle was challenged by Satan (the serpent of Genesis 3) in his temptation of the woman (Eve). She had rightly reaffirmed the principle when she acknowledged "You shall not eat from it or touch it, or you will die" (3:3). But the serpent (actually Satan behind a façade) flatly denied it this and asserted, "You surely will not die" (3:4). Satan even suggested a petty motive on God's part in withholding this one tree from the original

2 Leon Morris, *The Epistle to the Romans* (Grand Rapids, MI: Eerdmans, 1988), 287.

pair (3:5). Sadly, they both ate, and the consequence of their sin—the curse—fell on them (see Gen. 3:14–15 for the curse on the serpent; 3:16 for the curse on the woman). The curse on Adam reaffirmed the principle—sin means death, for he was told, You will "return to the ground, / Because from it you were taken, / for you are dust, / And to dust you shall return" (3:19).

This was the origin of what theologians call "original sin."

The Effect of Adam's Sin: Original Sin

The English poet John Donne was born in London in 1572. Educated, adventurous, and married young, Donne spent his early years living on the edge. His early poetry gave little indication of the deeply spiritual works for which he is better remembered today. In the years 1607 to 1610 Donne experienced a period of spiritual crisis brought on by disappointments, illnesses, and personal tragedy. Between 1612 and 1617 Donne's wife had one stillborn child, one miscarriage, two of their children died. In 1617 his wife Anne also died, at the age of 33. In 1615 he joined the Anglican clergy and in 1621 became the dean of St. Paul's church. Throughout his life he had endured numerous severe illnesses and in 1623 he became seriously ill with a relapsing, recurring, fever. One of his best-known works is titled *Devotions upon Emergent Occasions,* a work he wrote while on what he thought was his deathbed. Lying in bed, within earshot of the church, Donne could hear the church bells whenever there was a funeral service. Devotion 16 is titled "From the Bells of the Church Adjoining I am Daily Remembered of My Burial in the Funerals of Others." For Donne death was not some distant notion, or remote possibility—it was a daily reality, a certainty with memories and inevitability attached to it. Devotion 17 is titled "Now, This Bell Tolling Softly for Another, Says to Me: Thou Must Die." His point is not merely that he too must eventually die but that death, when it takes another person, takes a part of him as well. Donne wrote these famous lines to make this point:

> No man is an island, entire of itself; every man is a piece of the continent, a part of the main. If a clod be washed away by the sea, Europe is the less, as well as if a promontory were, as well as if a manor of thy friend's or of thine own were: any man's death diminishes me, because I am involved in mankind, and therefore never send to know for whom the bell tolls; it tolls for thee.

It is this very principle of corporate solidarity that Paul has in mind in Romans 5:12. The curse that fell on Adam (noted previously) did not just affect him. In Romans 5 the apostle Paul makes this stunning statement: "just as through one man sin entered the world, and death through sin, so death spread to all men, because all sinned" (Rom. 5:12). He repeats that point in Romans 5:18: "So then as through one transgression there resulted condemnation to all men." In First Corinthians 15:22 he yet again succinctly affirms, "For as in Adam all die."

Romans 5:12 reveals four facts about sin and death: first it reveals the source of sin in the world. The phrase "through one man sin entered into the world" points to the sin of Adam (Gen. 3; see previously). The second fact revealed in Romans 5:12 makes the connection between sin and death, "and death through sin." Here it is evident that death is the inevitable result of sin. Taken together these two facts lead to the third, the result of the connection is this, "and so death spread to all men." Here Paul reiterates another matter discussed already—everyone dies.

But this begs another question: If death is always the result of sin and everyone dies, does that mean everyone has sinned? That may seem obviously true (as Romans 3:23 affirms). But there is a problem. There are some people who die but have not actually sinned, such as infants or those whose mental development has not reached a level that they can be held responsible for their actions. Also, there are many who have not sinned against a direct commandment or rule such as Adam did in the Garden of Eden. Paul even seems to address this in Romans 5:14 "Nevertheless death reigned from Adam until Moses, even over those who had not sinned in the likeness of the offense of Adam." So, why do all those people die? The answer is the fourth fact of Romans 5:12: "because all sinned" in Adam. What this fact is revealing is that all die because all are guilty because of Adam's sin.

What the apostle Paul is teaching here is what theologians call "original sin" which is Adam's sin. That is, the "one man" Paul is referring to is Adam, and the last phrase of Romans 5:12 "because all sinned," means "because all sinned in Adam." (Paul is making the same point in First Corinthians 15:22, "in Adam all die.") Adam was placed in the Garden of Eden to be the head, the representative for all mankind that would come from him. When Adam, the representative of the entire human race fell, every human person that came from him became guilty. In short, all mankind is guilty because the head and representative of the human race sinned by eating the fruit of "the tree of the knowledge of good and evil."[3] "Mankind is a single entity, constituting a divinely ordered solidarity. Adam represents the entire human race that is descended from him. . . . Therefore, when Adam sinned, all mankind sinned."[4]

And so, the baneful list of Genesis 5 and the emphatic notation—"and he died," is traced back to Adam's sin as the words of the apostle Paul so simply, but sadly express it: "so death spread to all men." The author of Hebrews likewise makes the point simply: "it is appointed for men to die once" (Heb. 9:27).

Death Is Not Natural

One other point must be made here. Everything that has been said previously on the relation of sin and death presupposes that death was not a part of the original creation; sin was never meant to be part of the natural order

3 The full exposition of Romans 5 and a complete discussion of the doctrine of original sin in the human race is beyond the scope of this book. In brief, there are three main explanations of Paul's phrase "because all sinned." Some take this to mean "all have committed sins" and the meaning would then be "the death of each person (Rom.5:12) is caused by that person's own individual sinning" (Douglas Moo, *The Epistle to the Romans: The New International Commentary on the New Testament* [Grand Rapids, MI: Eerdmans, 1996], 323). We would expect, however, that if that were Paul's meaning he would have written "all are sinners." Even if it is fact that all are sinners this does not explain how Adam's sin and our sin are connected, which is Paul's point in Romans 5:12. "In other words, how can we logically relate the assertions 'each person dies because each person sins (in the course of history)' and 'one man's trespass has led to condemnation for all people' v. 18a?" (Moo, *Romans*, 323). Five times (5:15–19) Paul makes the point that because of "one man's sin" death reigned, and that man was Adam. So the fact that "death spread to all men" (5:12) is the result not of a string of individual sins but expressly "by the transgression of the one, death reigned through the one" (5:17). Another view is called the "realistic view," and simply asserts that the whole human race was "in Adam," in the sense that Levi was in Abraham, as in the argument of the author of Hebrews in Hebrews 7:9–10. This view is possible, but does not seem to fit well with the rest of Paul's arguments in Romans. The view taken in this book is the "representative view." This view argues that Adam was the representative (or "federal head") of the whole human race. As such his actions are "imputed" to (or "counted for," "credited to") the whole of his posterity—all humans after him. This view seems to be the best view, not least because it makes better sense of the parallel Paul makes with Christ in the rest of Romans 5. See the whole discussion in Moo, *Romans,* 326.

4 John MacArthur, *Romans 1–8: MacArthur New Testament Commentary* (Chicago: Moody Publishers, 1991), 293.

for mankind. When God completed His creation in six days, He "saw all that He had made and behold, it was very good" (Gen. 1:31). He could not have said this if death and corruption were already built into the creation.

The principle (noted earlier) "sin means death" has as its logical counterpart "no sin means no death." Before Adam's sin there was no sin, and so there was no death. Obviously, the original creation could be subject to death, because it was subjected to the sentence and penalty of death. But that the original creation was not necessarily subject to death is understood just because death is the penalty for sin. If there had been no sin, there would have been no penalty.

The warning of Genesis 2:17 is the first mention of death ("you will surely die") and states clearly that death would come from disobedience and sin. Theologian Geerhardus Johannes Vos states, "the belief of all ages has been that death is the penalty of sin, that the race became first subject to death through the commission of the primordial sin."[5]

Now, one might ask, "What if Adam had not sinned? Would he have lived forever?" That may seem to be a logical conclusion. That in turn begs these questions: *What would the world have looked like then? Would there be some of his race who sinned and died, and some, like him, who lived on? Would he have lived in the Garden of Eden forever?*

These "what if" questions may be interesting, but there is actually no way to answer them—and no need to answer them, because the historical fact is, Adam sinned and plunged the entire race of mankind into sin and death. The point to be affirmed here is that death must be understood as a penalty for sin. Again, the principle is "sin means death."

The Definition of Death: The Basic Idea—"Separation"

There is another question that arises from the Genesis 3 account. In Genesis 2:17 God told the man (Adam) "for in the day you eat from it [that is, from "the tree of the knowledge of good and evil"], you will surely die." And yet in Genesis 3, while the LORD God pronounces the sentence of death (that is, that Adam would "return to dust"—a euphemism for death and bodily decay) he did not die, but lived, had sons (as we have seen), and presumably (from the curse in Gen. 3:17–19), labored to grow food from the ground. So since Adam did not physically die on the day he ate from "the tree of the knowledge of good and evil," it seems God said one thing

5 Geerhardus Johannes Vos, *Biblical Theology: Old and New Testaments* (Edinburgh, UK: Banner of Truth, 1975), 36.

in Genesis 2:17 but did another in the curse of Genesis 3:19. Is there a contradiction here?

No, there is no contradiction, and to explain why that is so it will be necessary to understand the three kinds of death in the Bible.

The Three Kinds of Death

The quotation from Marcus Tullius Cicero (106 BC–43 BC), the great Roman statesman and philosopher, at the beginning of this chapter illustrates the truth that men have been trying to understand the nature and meaning of death for centuries—indeed, for millennia. But on their own they have arrived at no satisfactory answers; without God's Word, men have not been able to discover the meaning of death. As Hamlet observed, death is "the undiscovered country" from which "no traveler returns."[6] Only the Bible reveals the truth about death.

Physical Death

The biblical meaning of death is "separation." This is understood when one learns that, according to the Bible, there are actually three kinds of death. The first is, quite obviously, the death most familiar to everyone, namely, *physical* death, the separation of spirit from a body. This reality is behind the words of the Preacher in Ecclesiastes 12:7: "then the dust will return to the earth as it was, and the spirit will return to God who gave it." In James 2:26 this fact is simply stated, "the body without the spirit is dead." Matthew records that when Jesus died, He "cried out again with a loud voice, and yielded up His spirit" (Matt. 27:50). As Stephen was stoned to death he cried "Lord Jesus, receive my spirit!" (Acts 7:59). These instances reveal that at physical death, the spirit leaves the body, and the body returns "dust" (Gen. 3:19). In each of these texts, the idea is never that of annihilation of the person at death, but of the disintegration of the body and the on-going existence of the spirit. Thus, death is never annihilation (see Chapter 6).

Spiritual Death

The second kind of death is *spiritual* death, the separation of human beings from the Creator. This is the death the apostle Paul referred to in Ephesians 2 when he asserted that before the Ephesian believers were "made . . . alive together with Christ" (2:5), they "were dead in . . . trespasses and sins" (2:1)—

6 Shakespeare, *Hamlet*, Act III, Scene 1.

that is, they were separated by their sins from a holy and righteous God. Spiritual death is the "death" Adam suffered "in the day" he ate from "the tree of the knowledge of good and evil." The separation from God experienced by the first sinning pair is indicated by the fact that they "hid themselves from the presence of the LORD God among the trees of the garden" (Gen. 3:8). Furthermore, they lost the intimate fellowship with God they had enjoyed "walking in the garden in the cool of the day" (3:8), and they were driven from the garden (3:24). Eventually, as noted previously, both suffered physical death.

Eternal Death

The final kind of death is *eternal* death. This, too, is best understood as a "separation"—in this case, the permanent separation of the soul from God. It is when the separation of spiritual death is made into an eternal condition. This is the outcome Paul speaks of when he envisions God "dealing out retribution to those who do not know God and to those who do not obey the gospel of our Lord Jesus" (2 Thess. 1:8). Paul asserts "These will pay the penalty of eternal destruction, away from the presence of the Lord and from the glory of His power" (1:9). This is the "second death" the apostle John refers to in Revelation 20:14. This is the separation Jesus refers to in Matthew 25:41: "Then He will also say to those on His left, 'Depart from Me, accursed ones, into the eternal fire which has been prepared for the devil and his angels.'"

Study Questions:

1. What is the significance of the repetition of the phrase "and he died" in Genesis 5?
2. What is the full statement of the principle and meaning of "sin means death"?
3. What are the four facts about sin and death from Romans 5:12?
4. Define "original sin."
5. What is the basic idea of "death"?
6. Based on the answer to question #5, What are the three kinds of "death"?

2

What Happens after Death: Several Views

IN THE MOTION PICTURE *Gladiator* (2000), the main character is a Roman general turned Roman gladiator named Maximus. By misfortune Maximus finds himself at enmity with the Roman Emperor Commodus and narrowly escapes death: however his wife and son are killed by the vindictive and cruel, but powerful emperor. In the story, Maximus' life takes several unusual turns and his life is often threatened. While he seeks (and eventually achieves) vengeance on Commodus, his hope is seen in a final vision just before he dies. This vision is of a narrow gate through a solid stone fence, that leads to fields of ripe grain ready for harvest, under a sun-filled, but oddly hazy sky, to a road at the end of which is his wife and son waiting for him. This is the image of the Elysian Fields.

Ancient Greek Mythology: The Elysian Fields

The Elysian Fields, the Elysian Plains, or simply Elysium (terms which are commonly used, often in ways completely unrelated to the concept considered here), refers to a place of the mortal dead—a part of the underworld, according to ancient Greek mythology. The concept was never very clearly defined, probably because it was part of the shadowy and unknown world of the afterlife. It was at times seen as a beautiful island, a wide-open and produce-filled plain, or simply a garden that was a place of rest and refuge. It was seen as a place of rest and contentment, as opposed to Tartarus, the lowest place of the underworld, where the worst sinners are punished.

The writers of epic Greek mythology (Homer and Hesiod, among others), mention Elysium as a place favored by the gods where the heroes and demigods were allowed to go to avoid Hades; later Greek writers considered it a place where all who were not completely wicked would go after death. Virgil, a later Roman writer, mentions Elysium as a part of Hades (*Aeneid*, Book VI).

While a belief in the Elysian Fields as such is no longer the specific hope of many people, the idea that the afterlife holds the prospect of rest, contentment, and the reuniting of loved ones, is a generalized hope for many, even in the twenty-first century. However, that common conception is even less well-defined than that of the Elysian Fields, and the reasons for believing in it are just as hazy and vague.

MEDIEVAL ALLEGORY: *THE DIVINE COMEDY*

One of the great works of Western literature that deals, in a poetic and imaginative way, with this subject of life after death is *The Divine Comedy* by Dante Alighieri.[1] Written in Italian, this epic poem imaginatively describes a trip of the poet himself from hell to heaven, escorted by the Roman poet Virgil (author of *The Aeneid*); in the poem, Virgil represents human knowledge and wisdom. The poem is divided into three parts: Inferno, Purgatorio, and Paradiso.

In the first part, titled "Inferno," Dante and Virgil take a trip through hell. In Dante's imagination, hell is a place of danger for the poet and his escort (even though they are just passing through); ferocious animals (which symbolize human foibles) threaten to end their journey right there in hell. Dante's picture of hell consists of nine circles of various levels and types of judgment (and torture) that are consistent with the levels and types of sin.

The journey leads to a mountain island, the second part of the poem, "Purgatorio"; this, of course, represents purgatory. The mountain has seven terraces that represent the seven deadly sins, which must be overcome to continue the ascent. The ascent up the mountain is difficult, and at times painful, but only by such arduous effort can sin be overcome and the requisite virtue developed in order for travelers to make the necessary progress toward paradise.

In the final part of the poem, "Paradiso," Virgil (human wisdom) is left behind and Dante is escorted by Beatrice (the name of an actual woman known to Dante) who is idealized as divine wisdom. Heaven is depicted as consisting of nine celestial spheres (based on the ancient cosmology of Aristotle and Ptolemy). The spheres are where the cardinal virtues are refined; for instance, in the eighth sphere the highest religious virtues of faith, hope, and love are perfected. The ultimate goal is the "beatific vision," which is an indescribable spiritual perception of God (the Trinity) that fills the poet with divine love.

1 A good edition of this classic work is Dante Alighieri, *The Divine Comedy* (Oxford World's Classics), David H. Higgins, ed., C. H. Sisson, trans. (Oxford, UK: Oxford University Press: 2008).

To the surprise of some readers, many scholars believe that it is unlikely that Dante intended his readers to take his descriptions of hell, purgatory, and paradise (heaven) literally. *The Divine Comedy* is an allegory and was intended to describe the progress of a Medieval Christian soul in the world, through the vicissitudes of living the Christian life, seeking the "beatific vision." Thus, despite the apparently other-worldly titles for each part of *The Divine Comedy*, it is actually an allegory of life in this world for a medieval Christian, not the next life. In other words, the world itself—and life in it—has aspects of Inferno, Purgatorio, and Paradiso.

Reincarnation or Nirvana: The Buddhist View of the Afterlife

Buddhism teaches and the Buddhist believes that after a person dies he or she lives on.[2] This view of the afterlife is fairly simple (if not altogether clear), and there are only two basic possibilities: reincarnation (into a human body or perhaps a lower being—an animal or insect), or achieving *nirvana* (defined below). Which of these, and indeed, what sort of body into which one is re-born, depends on one's *karma*.

Karma is a principle or life force that one builds up in life, either for positive/good or negative/bad. If one lives well and develops positive *karma*, one's life turns out better and will lead to a better rebirth; conversely, if one lives poorly and develops negative *karma*, life turns out poorly and will lead to a lesser rebirth in the next life. With enough positive-*karma* lifetimes, one may even achieve *nirvana*.

Nirvana is a rather vague notion; it seems the Buddha did not define it very precisely, because he felt the focus should be on this life, not wistful thinking about the next. Nevertheless, *nirvana* is described as a state of being nothing (like a candle being "blown out") or "blissful oneness" with the universe and the end of all suffering and striving.

As stated, these ideas are rather vague (even in the Buddha's own teachings) and the Buddhist typically has few reasons why they should be believed. Often the rationale for believing in reincarnation or *nirvana* is simply that because one believes these things, he or she will be more aware of how he or she lives his or her life, so as to build up good, as opposed to bad, *karma*.

---

2 For a simple but good introduction to Buddhism, see Damien Keown, *Buddhism: A Very Short Introduction* (Oxford, UK: Oxford University Press, 1996); for a more detailed introduction to Buddhism, see Peter Harvey, *An Introduction to Buddhism: Teachings, History and Practices* (Introduction to Religion) Second Edition (Cambridge, UK: Cambridge University Press, 2012).

There is no biblical support, however, for either the notion of reincarnation or *nirvana*, and Hebrews 9:27 clearly says, "It is appointed for men to die once and after this comes judgment," leaving no room for the idea of reincarnation. Furthermore, the Bible teaches that all men (and women) are sinners—indeed, totally depraved (Jer. 17:9; Rom. 3:9–20; 7:14–24)—so that if the concept of *karma* was true, no human (with the exception of Jesus Christ [Heb. 4:15; 7:26]) would have any positive *karma*, but only negative *karma*.

Termination: The Materialist View

One of the most common views among many in secular Western culture is the belief that there is no afterlife. Materialists deny there is any immaterial or spiritual parts of reality or of human beings. For a materialist, the human brain is a remarkable substance where all thought and self-awareness reside, and when the brain dies, the mind of the person ceases to function and all thought and self-awareness cease. For many secular materialists this seems to be self-evidently true.

However, for many others it seems to be self-evidently true that there is an immaterial soul or spirit in every human being. Belief in the immaterial has been the view of the adherents of most major religions and societies of the world—from ancient times until now. Furthermore, even some thinkers in the materialist camp have conceded that a purely materialistic view of reality cannot adequately account for such undeniable features of human existence as self-consciousness and self-denying emotions like love. In short, the experiences and beliefs of millions of human beings that give testimony to a spiritual element in human souls makes it seem implausible (at least to them) to believe that there is no afterlife to look forward to or to dread.

Summary of the Views

These, of course, are not the only views of the afterlife. Virtually every religion ever conceived, from the ancient Egyptians to the tragic "Heaven's Gate" cult[3], has held to some form of belief in an afterlife. However, the

3 "On March 26, 1997, the bodies of 39 men and women were found in an opulent mansion outside San Diego, all victims of a mass suicide. Messages left by the Heaven's Gate group indicate that they believed they were stepping out of their 'physical containers' [i.e. their physical bodies] in order to ascend to a UFO that was arriving in the wake of the Hale-Bopp comet." George D. Chryssides, ed., *Heaven's Gate: Postmodernity and Popular Culture in a Suicide Group* (New York: Routledge, 2011), book abstract; no page number.

only reliable source for the truth about what happens after death is Scripture, because the Author of Scripture is the One who holds the power of life and death, and the life to come.

DEATH AND DIFFERENT ETERNAL DESTINIES

The three different types of death noted in Chapter 1, especially *eternal* death, point to divergent eternal destinies for the believer and unbeliever. As will be seen in later chapters, there is one destiny for those standing in righteousness before God and another for those who are called "the wicked," "the lost," the ones who die in a state of "spiritual death."

However, before considering those eternal destinies, it will be necessary in the next two chapters to discuss what may be called the "intermediate state." There are at least two reasons why a consideration of the "intermediate state" is necessary. For one thing, the teaching of the Bible on this subject is extensive, and yet, it does not directly address a number of questions. Furthermore, there are not a few who have attempted to answer those questions with speculation, superstition, or unbiblical ideas.

Study Questions:

1. What are "The Elysian Fields"?

2. What are the three parts of *The Divine Comedy* by Dante Alighieri and what kind of literature is this book?

3. What is the Buddhist view of *nirvana*?

4. Why do these views fail to provide any reliable truth about the afterlife?

3

The Intermediate State, Part I:

Death and the Intermediate State

THE SIXTEENTH CHAPTER of Luke records an unusual parable of Jesus (Luke 16:19–31). Found only in Luke's Gospel, it is the only one of Jesus' parables in which He gives a name to a character. And it is unusual in terms of the details it describes, if not the lesson it teaches. It is the parable of the rich man and Lazarus.

> Now there was a rich man, and he habitually dressed in purple and fine linen, joyously living in splendor every day. And a poor man named Lazarus was laid at his gate, covered with sores, and longing to be fed from the crumbs which were falling from the rich man's table; besides, even the dogs were coming and licking his sores. Now the poor man died and was carried away by the angels to Abraham's bosom; and the rich man also died and was buried. In Hades he raised his eyes, being in torment, and saw Abraham far away and Lazarus in his bosom. And he cried out and said, "Father Abraham, have mercy on me, and send Lazarus so that he may dip the tip of his finger in water and cool off my tongue, for I am in agony in this flame." But Abraham said, "Child, remember that during your life you received your good things, and likewise Lazarus bad things; but now he is being comforted here, and you are in agony. And besides all this, between us and you there is a great chasm fixed, so that those who wish to come over from here to you will not be able, and that none may cross over from there to us." And he said, "Then I beg you, father, that you send him to my father's house—for I have five brothers—in order that he may warn them, that they will not also come to this place of torment." But Abraham said, "They have Moses and the Prophets; let them hear them." But he said, "No, father Abraham, but if someone goes to them from the dead, they will repent!" But he said to him, "If they do not listen to Moses and the Prophets, they will not be persuaded even if someone rises from the dead."

This parable[1] has two main characters and two "scenes"—one brief and introductory, relating the life of the two men; the other describing the "afterlife" of the two main characters. The first scene—of life—identifies the men. The first is described as "rich" and "habitually dressed in purple and fine linen," who was "enjoying himself in splendor every day."

In later tradition, this rich man is given the name "Dives" (a Latin term for "wealthy"), but the fact is, Jesus never identified the man by name—and that is significant. The "rich man" clearly enjoyed "the good life" and was much like the rich man in the parable in Luke 12:16–21, who had wealth in this life, but was unprepared for the next life. He had so much in this life, but he took none of it into the afterlife—not even his name! When he died, he was buried.

In contrast, the life of the second man, Lazarus, was miserable. He was "poor"—destitute, in fact. He suffered from a disease that produced sores over his whole body—running sores, apparently, because they attracted dogs that licked at them. (These were not household pets, but scavenger dogs—disease-ridden strays.) He was possibly crippled, because it says he "was laid" at the rich man's gate. Lazarus survived on "the crumbs which were falling from the rich man's table." Make no mistake, these were not the leftovers of a meal, graciously and intentionally donated to the destitute man; these scraps were the *garbage* left from the rich man's banquets. When he died, in contrast to the rich man, he "was carried away by the angels to Abraham's bosom."

The expression "Abraham's bosom" is found in the 1995 NASB and in the KJV. The word for "bosom" (translated "arms" in the 2020 NASB) is *kolpos* and refers to someone's side or lap. This is the only place in the Bible where this expression is found and it is unknown elsewhere in first-century Judaism, although Fourth Maccabees 13:17 and possibly First Kings 1:21, 2:10, and 11:21 may convey a similar idea.[2]

In the second scene—in the afterlife—the circumstances of "life" for both men is completely reversed. The rich man finds himself "in Hades," "in torment," "in agony" from fire ("flames") that surrounded him. The term "Hades" refers to the place of the dead in Greek myth and in common expression (see more on Hades later in this chapter). In the Greek version of the Old

---

1 There is debate over whether this story should be considered a parable at all. However, Robert H. Stein, in a chapter that asks the question, "What Is a Parable?" includes this story in a list of "Stories That Are Clearly Parables" (Robert H. Stein, *An Introduction to the Parables of Jesus* [Philadelphia: Westminster Press, 1981]).

2 Robert H. Stein, *Luke: The New American Commentary* (Nashville, TN: Broadman & Holman Publishers, 1992), 424.

Testament (LXX) it was used to translate Sheol (see more on Sheol later in this chapter). In the Old Testament it can mean the place of the dead or the place where the unrighteous dead go, in contrast with "heaven" (Ps. 139:8; Amos 9:2). In this parable it clearly refers to the place of the unrighteous dead in contrast to "Abraham's bosom"—the place of the righteous dead.

In this scene another character is introduced—Abraham himself. While the rich man can see that Lazarus was "being comforted," while he was "in agony," he apparently was not able to speak to Lazarus directly. So he makes a request of Abraham to send Lazarus with some relief. But this is rejected by Abraham for two reasons. One is that the rich man had enjoyed his luxury in life while Lazarus suffered—so now Lazarus is enjoying the comfort he did not have in life. And the other reason is that "a great chasm has been set, so that those who want to go over from here to you will not be able, nor will any people cross over from there to us." The term "chasm" is found only here and indicates an unbridgeable space.[3]

The rich man makes a further request—he wants to have Lazarus sent back to warn his brothers so that they will avoid his torment. But Abraham explains that this is impossible and unnecessary because the living "have Moses and the Prophets."

What Does This Parable Teach about the Afterlife?

It is necessary to be cautious when seeking information on the afterlife from this parable. For one thing, it is just that, namely a parable. That is, Jesus was not—in the first instance—intending to teach about the terrain of the under-world, or the conditions of the afterlife. It may be allowed that some general inferences may legitimately be drawn from the second scene—in the afterlife—in which He describes of the afterlife for both men; but the parable is told as a warning to those still living (that is, in the first scene—in life) not primarily as a window into the environment of the afterlife. In short, there are elements of the parable that are unlikely to be true of the afterlife of either the righteous or the wicked.

For instance, in the parable after his death Lazarus was "carried away by the angels to Abraham's bosom." On the basis of this passage some have

3 "The theological passive that such a place 'has been fixed' asserts that God has set up the afterlife in such a way that the righteous and the unrighteous do not mix. . . . The image is strong and suggests that how we respond in this life is decisive for where we reside in the next" (Darrell L. Bock, *Luke 9:51–24:53: Baker Exegetical Commentary on the New Testament* [Grand Rapids, MI; Baker Academic, 1996], 1373).

taught that all those who believe in Jesus will be transported to heaven by angels. However, this is the only text in the Bible that makes such a suggestion, and other passages teach that the believer, at physical death, simply enters the presence of the Lord (2 Cor. 5:8; see more on this in Chapter 4). Also, as noted, this is the only text that speaks of "Abraham's bosom" (KJV). However, this is better rendered "Abraham's arms" (as in the 2020 NASB) and should be understood as an indication of a place of care, comfort, and rest. While the parable shows that the rich man saw Lazarus actually being embraced by Abraham, this should be taken as a part of the symbolic and metaphorical image of the parable as a whole—not a promise that all the righteous dead will be physically embraced (by Abraham).

In the parable the rich man is able to see Lazarus and converse with Abraham. However, this too seems to be a feature of the parable that is found in no other passages concerning the afterlife. As will be noted later, the texts that do indicate the abode of the unrighteous after death seem to refer to it as a place of silence (Ps. 94:17—"If the LORD had not been my help, / My soul would soon have dwelt in the abode of silence"; 115:17—"The dead do not praise the LORD, / Nor do any who go down into silence"; 31:17—"Let the wicked be put to shame, let them be silent in Sheol"). Scripture also calls it a place of darkness (Job 10:21–22—"To the land of darkness and deep shadow, / The land of utter gloom as darkness itself, / Of deep shadow without order, / And which shines as the darkness"). This seems to indicate that the elements of the parable (such as interaction and conversation between the rich man and Abraham) are included only to serve the main point of the parable, not to inform the reader of possible conditions in the afterlife. Indeed, it seems that if the detail of the "great chasm" is meant to convey anything about the afterlife, it is meant to convey that interaction and conversation between residents of the two sides cannot happen.

What, then, *can* be learned about the afterlife from this parable? The whole premise of the parable is that there will be a reckoning in the afterlife based on what was experienced or done in life. That is, for this parable to be a warning to the wicked, and/or a comfort to the righteous, there must actually be an afterlife appropriate to each—rest and comfort to the righteous and torment for the wicked. Clearly, Jesus wanted His hearers to consider that eventuality and to live accordingly. Beyond that, information about the intermediate and eternal destinies of the wicked and the righteous will have to be gained from other texts in the Bible.

The Mystery of the Intermediate State

Sheol

Many questions about the intermediate state are linked to the meaning of the Old Testament conception of Sheol; this term is a transliteration of a Hebrew term (*šĕʾôl*) that has a number of connotations and nuances.

In general, the term Sheol refers to the grave, the place of burial of the dead, which is in a physical sense the abode of the dead. However, it can also indicate a place beyond the grave or tomb of the body, denoting a place for the departed spirits of men.

In Psalm 88 the psalmist laments that his troubles have brought him to the point where his "life has drawn near to Sheol" (88:3); he laments further (using Hebrew poetic parallelism),

> I am reckoned among those who go down to the pit;
> I have become like a man without strength,
> Forsaken among the dead,
> Like the slain who lie in the grave,
> Whom You [He is speaking to the Lord, 88:1] remember no more,
> And they are cut off from Your hand.
> You have put me in the lowest pit,
> In dark places, in the depths. (88:4–6)

Here the Psalmist links the terms "Sheol," "grave," and "pit." The term "grave" (Hebrew, *qeber*) indicates a "sepulcher" or "burial site" as in Genesis 23:9 and 20, where Abraham purchases a plot of ground to bury Sarah. The term "pit" (Hebrew, *bowr*) indicates something like a cistern or even simply a hole in the ground, as in Genesis 37:22, 24, and 29, where the sons of Jacob put Joseph. The term is also used in Genesis 40:15 and 41:14, where it is rendered "dungeon." Thus, for the psalmist, Sheol is associated with the grave and other places "down," beneath the surface of the earth.

The Old Testament frequently indicates that Sheol is located "down," in places of depth, in the lower parts of the earth (Deut. 32:22; 1 Sam. 28:11–15; Job 26:5; Ps. 86:13; Isa. 7:11; Ezek. 31:14–18). Jacob's expression, "I will go down to Sheol in mourning/sorrow" (Gen. 37:35; 42:38; 44:29, 31), refers in each instance to Jacob's death from remorse for his lost son(s).

Descriptions of this place of the dead in the Old Testament are bleak. It is unavoidable; the Psalmist in Psalm 89:14 asks two rhetorical questions: "What man can live and not see death? Can he deliver his soul from the power of Sheol?" The answers are "No one" to the first question and "No" to the second. The prophet Isaiah describes Sheol in terms of a devouring beast: "Therefore Sheol has enlarged its throat and opened its mouth without measure" (Isa. 5:14; see also Prov. 1:12; 27:20).

Sheol is not a place beyond the reach of God. God knows it very well: "Naked is Sheol before Him" (Job 26:6); "Sheol . . . lie[s] open before the LORD" (Prov. 15:11); and Psalm 139:8 simply affirms that even in Sheol, He is there. No one can hide from God in Sheol (Amos 9:2). Sheol is the place the LORD takes people (1 Sam. 2:6) and His anger burns there (Deut. 32:22); therefore, Job's request to hide from God's wrath in Sheol (Job 14:13) is futile. One does not escape from God by going to Sheol.

The book of Job pictures it as a place without hope (17:14–15) and a place of gloom and darkness (10:21–22; 17:13; see also Ps. 143:3). The preacher/author of Ecclesiastes describes it as a place without love, hate, envy, work, thought, knowledge, or wisdom (9:5–6) and a place without meaningful activity (9:10). In the Psalms it is described as a place of silence (94:17) where the LORD is not praised (115:17; 6:5; 88:10). Job calls it a place of trembling (26:5) and a place of no return: "When a cloud vanishes, it is gone; / In the same way one who goes down to Sheol does not come up. / He will not return to his house again, / Nor will his place know him anymore" (7:9–10; 10:21).

A number of texts describe this as the place where the wicked and sinners will go (21:13; 24:19; Ps. 5:5; 7:27; 9:17; 31:17; 49:14; 55:15). Of course, as noted, all die and go to the "grave," however, although "the righteous go to the grave (Sheol) they are delivered from it, whereas the wicked remain there."[4] In Psalm 49 the psalmist affirms that the foolish are "appointed for Sheol; Death shall be their shepherd . . . And their form shall be for Sheol to consume" (49:14). But this psalmist is confident that "God will redeem my soul from the power of Sheol, For He will receive me" (49:15).

This seems to be the same sentiment of the prophet Hosea. In Hosea 13:14 the NASB has two rhetorical questions: "Shall I ransom them from the power of Sheol? Shall I redeem them from death?" However, these phrases "are better interpreted as declarations" that "God will indeed ransom and redeem Israel from death."[5] Thus the other rhetorical questions in Hosea 13:14—"O Death, where are your thorns? O Sheol, where is your sting?"—

---

4 W.A. Van Gemeren, "Sheol," *Evangelical Dictionary of Theology*, ed. Walter A. Elwell (Grand Rapids, MI, Baker: 2001), 1099.

5 John K. Goodrich, "Hosea," in *The Moody Bible Commentary*, ed. Michael Rydelnik and Michael Vanlaningham (Chicago, IL: Moody Publishers, 2014), 1328.

are taunts against the pain and fear of Death and Sheol, "because they posed no permanent threat to Israel."[6] The apostle Paul quotes Hosea 13:14 in First Corinthians 15:55, and in doing so affirms that for the believer (as for the Savior, Psalm 16:10) the Lord will not abandon the righteous to Sheol. The believer can claim the promise of Psalm 86:13: "For Your lovingkindness toward me is great, / And You have delivered my soul from the depths of Sheol." The path of life leads "away from Sheol" (Prov. 15:24).

Hades

Another term used in the Bible that raises another set of questions about the intermediate state is the term *Hades*. "The word Sheol was translated into Greek as *hadēs* sixty-one times in the LXX," and the term itself "occurs ten times in the NT."[7] Hades is a term used in secular Greek literature—particularly in Greek mythology—but it would be a mistake to import any aspects of the Greek mythological meaning or significance of Hades into the use of that term in either the Old or New Testaments.

In the Gospels the Greek term Hades appears in Jesus' condemnation of Capernaum: "And you, Capernaum, will not be exalted to heaven, will you? You will descend to Hades" (Matt. 11:23). Here it is clear that Hades and heaven are opposite destinies for people. In Matthew 16:18, when Jesus promises to "build My church," He adds the assurance "and the gates of Hades will not overpower it."

Jesus' reference to Hades in this verse is a figure of speech called *metonymy*, where something (in this case, Hades) is used to represent something else closely associated with it (in this case, Satan and his demons). This is similar to instances in Scripture where heaven is used to speak of God. Jesus is saying that Satan and the demons—the ones who are the most prominently associated with that place of torment—are the ones who stand in opposition to, but will not prevail over, the church.

In Peter's sermon on the day of Pentecost, the apostle quotes Psalm 16:10: "Because You will not abandon my soul to Hades, Nor allow Your Holy One to undergo decay" (Acts 2:27). These are the words of David written in a poetic and hyperbolic way, affirming his trust in the preserving grace of the Lord (Ps. 16:5–11). Peter applies these words literally to Jesus' resurrection from the dead (Acts 2:24). The apostle acknowledges that the words of the Psalm could not be literally applied to David: "Brethren, I may

6 Goodrich, "Hosea."

7 Van Gemeren, "Sheol," 1099.

confidently say to you regarding the patriarch David that he both died and was buried, and his tomb is with us to this day" (Acts 2:29). Peter even goes so far as to argue that David wrote those words prophetically of the resurrection of Jesus: "And so, because he was a prophet and knew that God had sworn to him with an oath to seat one of his descendants on his throne, he looked ahead and spoke of the resurrection of the Christ" (2:30–31). It was because of His resurrection that Jesus did not go to Hades.

The Greek term "Hades" in Acts 2:27 and 31 is the Hebrew term "Sheol" in Psalm 16:10. As noted previously, the term "Sheol" often simply indicates the grave, but can denote a place for the departed spirits of men. Here in Acts 2 it is clear that while Jesus was temporarily placed in a tomb or grave, He was delivered from Hades/Sheol in that not only did His body not languish and decay in the tomb, but He was delivered from that place of torment, of darkness and gloom, of hopelessness and abandonment from God.

In Revelation, the term Hades is used four times. First, in John's great vision of the risen and glorified One, Christ identifies Himself: "I am the first and the last, and the living One; and I was dead, and behold, I am alive forevermore, and I have the keys of death and of Hades" (Rev. 1:17–18). Here He is claiming that by His death and resurrection He has defeated death (1 Cor. 15:54–57) and overcome the power of Hades. He has provided a way out (as keys are used to unlock doors) to avoid Hades and its torments and loss.

Second, in Revelation 6:8, Hades appears as an accompaniment of death, reiterating the connection between death and the place where the unbelieving must go after death.

Third, in Revelation 20, the scene in view here is the judgment by One sitting on a "great white throne" (Rev. 20:11). This is the judgment of all "the dead, the great and the small" (20:12), all those whose names were "not found written in the book of life" (20:15)—that is, all the unbelieving from all the ages of the earth. This judgment results in the final judgment of the "lake of fire." The dead who are judged are resurrected from the sea: "And the sea gave up the dead which were in it" and both "death and Hades gave up the dead which were in them" (20:13).

Fourth, a most significant statement about Hades is revealed in 20:14: "Then death and Hades were thrown into the lake of fire. This is the second death, the lake of fire." Here it seems that Hades is an intermediate place for the unbelieving dead, that will itself be cast into the ultimate place of final judgment, the "lake of fire."

Study Questions:

1. What does "bosom" literally mean in the phrase "Abraham's bosom," and how is "Abraham's bosom" used in the parable in Luke 16:19–31?

2. Why must readers be cautious when using the parable in Luke 16:19–31 to learn about the afterlife?

3. According to this parable (and Jesus' teaching) what is a better source of truth about the afterlife than someone rising from the dead to speak to the living? Why would that be so?

4. What is the basic meaning of "Sheol"? Why does that meaning lend itself to picturing the afterlife? What are the conditions in "Sheol"?

5. What is the basic meaning of "Hades"? Why does that meaning lend itself to picturing the afterlife? What are the conditions in "Hades"?

4

The Intermediate State, Part II:
Non-Biblical Views and Misconceptions of the Intermediate State

IN MANY TOWNS, SMALL and large, a common feature is the local cemetery, with headstones or plaques of various sizes and the names and dates (birth and death) of the "residents" there. These graveyards are often given euphemistic names—"Pleasant Valley," "Restful Acres," and "Memorial Gardens," among others—intended to suggest that the residents are in a place of bucolic rest, separated from the stresses of life, and enjoying a feeling of quiet peace and repose. Those buried there are said to be "laid to rest." And on many a headstone is the inscription *R.I.P.*—which of course stands for "Rest in Peace."

Do the Dead Really "Rest in Peace"?

All of this is intended to convey the notion that the deceased are really just resting, in a state of inactivity and ease, as if they were merely asleep. Indeed, the very term "cemetery" comes from the Latin term *coemeterium*, which is itself came from the Greek word *koimeterion*, "sleeping place or dormitory." In short, the very word "cemetery" suggests the idea that those who reside there are only asleep.

It is not difficult, then, to understand why people often speak of the dead as those who are "asleep." In preparation for burial the deceased are usually placed in a reclining position, with eyes closed and often with hands folded across the breast—very much as they were when they were alive, but only sleeping. The Bible itself uses such language; for instance, Jesus used the euphemism of sleep for Lazarus in John 11:11, when He knew Lazarus was dead (11:14). The same euphemism is used of Stephen as he died (Acts 7:60) and of believers who have died but will rise at the rapture of the church (1 Cor. 15:6, 18, 20, 51; 1 Thess. 4:13–15; see also the discussion in Chapter 10). From this some have taught the doctrine of "soul sleep."

Soul Sleep

Perhaps the best way to better understand the doctrine of "soul sleep" is to present a series of questions about this doctrine, with answers that will expound and explain this belief.

What is the concept (or doctrine) of "soul sleep"?

The use of the euphemism of "sleep" when speaking of the dead has led some to a doctrine of "soul sleep." This doctrine is a way of addressing the questions that concern the intermediate state.

In effect, this doctrine teaches that the intermediate state is an unconscious state very much like normal sleep. Although there are some variations of this idea, the basic idea is that at the moment of death a person enters a state that is like natural sleep (apart from dreaming—a brain activity) in which there is no awareness or consciousness; it is very like a state of suspended animation. Instead, the dead are "asleep" and waiting for the day when they "wake up." It is the unconsciousness and inactivity of the bodily state of sleeping that seems to be an apt way to describe the unconsciousness and inactivity of the intermediate state.

Where did the concept of "soul sleep" originate?

In some respects, this notion seems to arise almost naturally from the way, as noted, the bodies of the dead are spoken of and treated in the preparation and process of burial. Also, as noted, this euphemism is used in the New Testament. When the euphemism is taken literally the doctrine of "soul sleep" seems to have some credibility.

There were some in the early church who taught something like "soul sleep" as early as the second century.[1] Later, there were some in "radical reformation"[2] (i.e., Anabaptists) and even Socinians that held to this doctrine. Contemporary groups that teach some version of "soul sleep" include the Seventh-Day Adventists, Jehovah's Witnesses, and Christadelphians.

1 See Jeremiah Mutie, *Death in Second Century Christian Thought* (Eugene, OR: Pickwick Publications, 2015) 60–62.

2 The expression "radical reformation" is not meant to be judgmental in any way. The sense of the term "radical" here does not convey something "extreme" but is used in the sense of "from/to the roots" (Latin: *radix*). This branch of the reformation wanted to get back the "roots" of Christian practice—i.e., simple services, two ordinances. This terminology is the standard (non-pejorative) way to refer to these groups in many texts of church history.

Why is the concept of "soul sleep" not viable?

While the conceptual move from the biblical euphemism of "sleep" for "death" to a doctrine of "soul sleep" is comprehensible, such a move is unwarranted. As noted, this doctrine maintains that in the state of "soul sleep" a person is unconscious and inactive; however, several texts of the Bible indicate this is not the case.

First, there are passages that indicate that there will be conscious fellowship with God after death. When Jesus made the promise to the thief on the cross next to His—"Truly I say to you, today you will be with Me in Paradise" (Luke 23:43)—He clearly implied an immediate and conscious fellowship between Himself and the thief. When Stephen, at the moment of his death (and echoing the words of His Lord, Luke 23:46), cried out, "Lord Jesus, receive my spirit!" (Acts 7:59), he anticipated precisely what Jesus promised the thief—an immediate and conscious fellowship with Jesus. This is exactly what Paul indicates to the Corinthians when he assures them that "to be absent from the body" is "to be at home with the Lord" (2 Cor. 5:8).

Second, there are other passages, such as in the book of Revelation, where the dead are conscious and active in heaven. In Revelation 7, John identifies the multitude in heaven that worships God:

> After these things I looked, and behold, a great multitude which no one could count, from every nation and all the tribes, peoples, and languages, standing before the throne and before the Lamb, clothed in white robes, and palm branches were in their hands; and they cried out with a loud voice, saying, "Salvation belongs to our God who sits on the throne, and to the Lamb." (Rev. 7:9–10)

These are men and women, believers, the martyrs of the tribulation: "These are the ones who come out of the great tribulation, and they have washed their robes and made them white in the blood of the Lamb." (7:14). They are distinguished from the angels and other heavenly creatures (7:11). They are most certainly dead, being martyrs, but they join the angels, the twenty-four elders (4:4, 10; 5:8) and "the four living creatures" (4:6, 8; 5:6; 6:1, 6; 7:11) in worship and praise of God (7:11–12). Clearly, these saints are not unconscious or inactive while they await the resurrection. This is true also of the twenty-four elders, who are themselves distinguished from the angels and heavenly creatures and are quite conscious and active.[3]

---

3 The identification of these "elders" as such probably indicates that they are representative of the church. See John MacArthur, *Because the Time is Near* (Chicago: Moody Publishers, 2007), 110–112.

Furthermore, from these texts, it seems clear that the euphemism of "sleep" for the dead pertains to the body and not the soul. In the two main texts (1 Cor. 15:50–57; 1 Thess. 4:13–18) where Paul uses this euphemism, he teaches that those "asleep" are to be "raised imperishable" (1 Cor. 15:52). In First Thessalonians 4:16 Paul says "the dead"—clearly referring to those who are identified earlier in the context as "those who are asleep" (4:13–14)—will "rise first." In short, it is at the resurrection of the body that the "sleep" ends. The souls of these saints are said to be coming with Him—which makes sense only if they were, in some sense, aware and in fellowship with Him (as Second Corinthians 5:8 teaches) before the event of the resurrection of the body. Here it becomes most obvious that the euphemism is just that—not to be taken literally, because that which "sleeps" is the body, which is not just inactive, but has ceased to function at all.

In summary, while the doctrine of "soul sleep" has a superficial plausibility, it must be judged to be unbiblical and false. The Christian does not anticipate an indeterminate time of slumber after death but an immediate experience of indescribable joy (and gain, Phil. 1:21) in the very presence of his or her Lord, Jesus Christ (2 Cor. 5:8).

PURGATORY

Purgatory is another unbiblical view of the intermediate state, understood as a place of judgment on persons who are destined for heaven (or the "beatific vision"), but are not yet possessed of sufficient righteousness or spiritual merit. Those persons who "die in God's grace and friendship" but are "imperfectly purified" can be sure of going to heaven—eventually—but must "undergo purification" so that they may achieve the holiness necessary to "enter the joy of heaven."[4]

In Roman Catholic doctrine, purgatory is a place where those who have died in a state of grace (that is, free from mortal sin) and in friendship with God, but who still lack the requisite holiness for heaven due to the presence of venial sin (likened to a stain or illness; as opposed to a mortal sin, which is a sin that has destroyed sanctifying grace) is "purged," that is, expiated, cleansed, or purified through punishment visited on the offending believer or by works of the living on behalf of the dead, such as almsgiving, indulgences,

4 Roman Catholic Church, *Catechism of the Catholic Church*, 2nd ed. (Washington, DC: United States Catholic Conference, 2000), 328.

and works of penance.[5] This judgment of purgatory is expected to be severe punishment that can last for a considerable time (even thousands of years) but will eventually lead to a matriculation to heaven.

The Origin of the Doctrine of Purgatory: Parallel Concepts

There have been other traditions and religions that envision something like purgatory for the dead. For instance, Buddhism teaches that there are "fiery realms" that sound like hell to those in the Christian traditions, but actually seem to function like purgatory; those relegated to those realms are eventually released (reincarnated) after their negative *karma* has run its course. Buddhists also offer prayers for the dead, but the intent of such prayers is not like those offered on behalf of souls in purgatory in Roman Catholicism.

Like Buddhists, Hindus believe in *Naraka* or *Yamaloka*, a location in the underworld where humans suffer for their sins in this life. There are many levels of this place of pain and suffering; the god of death, *Yama*, assigns the dead to the level of punishment appropriate to their sins. The entire system is complex and confused, with textual authorities in Hinduism offering contradictory descriptions and conditions. What seems to be clear is that, given the Hindu doctrine of reincarnation, *Naraka* is not a permanent state. However, it is not clear that the purpose of the suffering in *Naraka* is "purifying," as in the Catholic understanding of purgatory.

At one place in his dialogue *Gorgias*, Plato discusses the punishments the dead will undergo in the afterlife. Here he offers a vision of differences in the punishments the dead will have to endure. On the one hand, someone guilty of great crimes and "many and terrible deeds of sacrilege, murders foul and violent" would be cast into Tartarus[6]—never to be released. On the other hand, "Those again who have committed crimes, which, although great, are not irremediable—who in a moment of anger, for example, have done violence to a father or a mother, and have repented for the remainder of their lives, or who have taken the life of another under the like extenuating circumstances" will be "plunged into Tartarus" however, the pains of which they are compelled to undergo last "for a year, but at the end of the year" they are expelled. This is an interesting comment on the afterlife by the great philosopher, but it is quite brief and does not seem to describe the same environment or rationale for the punishment in the Catholic elucidation of purgatory.

5 Catechism of the Catholic Church, 328.

6 Second Peter 2:4 uses the verb form *tartaroó*, "to cast into tartarus"; here the idea is that this is the place of punishment for fallen angels.

Other proposed precursors to the Western notions of purgatory can be found in Greek and Roman mythologies, especially those that relate purported accounts of the underworld. One notable example can be found in Book VI of The Aeneid by the Roman poet Virgil, "The World Below."[7] Here the intrepid Aeneas visits the underworld and sees all manner of lamentation of the dead and various forms of "purgatory-like" punishments of those who "put off atonements in the world." The dead in some cases are waiting for a chance to move on to other stages of the afterlife which happens only after "they flutter and roam this side a hundred years."[8]

Yet none of these parallel instances of a "purgatory-like" state after death can be said to be the origin of purgatory as it came to be conceived in Catholic theology.

The Roman Catholic Doctrine: Sources of the Doctrine

Those who defend the Roman Catholic idea of purgatory claim that the sources for this doctrine can be found in the church fathers, the Bible, and other tradition. Furthermore, Catholics will appeal to important theologians as well as the determinations of church councils (e.g., the Council of Trent 1545, 1563).

Where do Catholics see purgatory in the Church Fathers?

Clement of Alexandria, in his *Stromata* (Book 4, 24 "The Reason and End of Divine Punishments") teaches that there are "two methods of correction — the instructive (*didaskalikos*) and the punitive (*kolastikos*) which we have called the disciplinary."[9] The sins committed before baptism are not subject to discipline for they "are remitted," but the sins committed after baptism "are purged." While Clement likely has the discipline in this life in view, he is indicating here the principle of "purging sin" from those who are already baptized.

In a sermon on Job 1:5, the church father John Chrysostom (c. 347–407) defended the notion of sacrifices for the dead[10] with this comment: "If

7 Robert Fitzgerald, trans., *The Aeneid: Virgil* (New York: Vintage Classics, 1990), 157–92.

8 Ibid, 179; Book VI line 765; 171; Book VI line 445.

9 Peter Kirby, ed., "Clement of Alexandria, Stromata, Book 4," *Early Christian Writings*, http://www.earlychristianwritings.com/text/clement-stromata-book4.html accessed September 20, 2022.

10 See St. John Chrysostom, *Hom. In 1 Cor. 41*, J.-P Migne, *Patrologia cursus completes series Graeca*, 162 vols. (Paris, 1857–66), 61, 361.

Job's sons were purified by their father's sacrifice, why would we doubt that our offerings for the dead bring them some consolation? Let us not hesitate to help those who have died and to offer our prayers for them."[11]

Catholics also appeal to the works of Gregory the Great (in his *Dialogues*, Book 4, chapter 39) and to the canons of the Council of Trent 1563 (*Canons and Decrees of the Council of Trent*/Session XXV/Purgatory).[12]

Where do Catholics see purgatory in the Apocryphal Books?

A key text that Catholics cite in support for the doctrine of purgatory is found in Second Maccabees 12:45 that says, "Therefore he [speaking of Judas Maccabeus] made atonement for the dead, so that they might be delivered from their sin."

In order to better analyze this text, the whole context should be cited:

> On the next day, as had now become necessary, Judas and his men went to take up the bodies of the fallen and to bring them back to lie with their kindred in the sepulchres of their fathers. Then under the tunic of each one of the dead they found sacred tokens of the idols of Jam'nia, which the law forbids the Jews to wear. And it became clear to all that this was why these men had fallen. So they all blessed the ways of the Lord, the righteous Judge, who reveals the things that are hidden; and they turned to prayer, beseeching that the sin that had been committed might be wholly blotted out. The noble Judas exhorted the people to keep themselves free from sin, for they had seen with their own eyes what had happened because of the sin of those who had fallen. He also took up a collection, man by man, to the amount of two thousand drachmas of silver, and sent it to Jerusalem to provide for a sin offering. In doing this he acted very well and honorably, taking account of the resurrection. For if he were not expecting that those who had fallen would rise again, it would have been superfluous and foolish to pray for the dead. But if he was looking to the splendid reward that is laid up for those who fall asleep in godliness, it was a holy and pious thought. Therefore he made atonement for the dead, so that they might be delivered from their sin."[13]

According to this account, after a great but costly victory Judas Maccabeus sent his surviving soldiers to bury the bodies of their fallen comrades.

---

11 Cited in Catechism of the Catholic Church, 328; the paragraph is 1032.

12 Catechism of the Catholic Church, 328.

13 Second Maccabees 12:39–45, cited from the New Revised Standard Version Bible: Catholic Edition (New York: HarperOne, 1993), 1331.

In the course of this exercise they discovered that all of them had carried idols under their tunics. (It was this idolatry that had led to their deaths.) However, the survivors desired to honor the fallen nevertheless and in that spirit Judas took up a collection to send to Jerusalem to "provide for a sin offering." The author of this book added the commentary that in "doing this he acted very well and honorably" because this indicated that he believed in the resurrection of the dead. Thus, the author commends Judas' prayers and offerings for the dead because "he was looking to the splendid reward that is laid up for those who fall asleep in godliness [which was] a holy and pious thought. Therefore he made atonement for the dead, that they might be delivered from their sin." (2 Macc. 12:45).

It should be noted that while the author of Second Maccabees apparently approves of the notion of prayers and offerings for the dead, there are no other references to this practice in the other books of the Apocrypha and this practice finds no support at all in any canonical books of the Old Testament.

Furthermore, this passage makes no explicit reference to purgatory. And it should be noted this text actually contradicts the explicit Catholic doctrine of purgatory because the men for whom the prayers and offerings were made had died as idolaters, not in a state of grace and friendship with God. Indeed, Second Maccabees 12:40 explicitly states that their idolatry "was the reason these men had fallen." Also, the second commandment forbids idolatry (Exod. 20:4; Deut. 5:8–11) and the penalty for idolatry was severe, up to and including death (17:1–7).

Where do Catholics see purgatory in the Canon of the New Testament?

In defending the doctrine of purgatory, Catholic theologians point to several passages in the New Testament. For instance, the apostle Paul writes: "each man's work will become evident; for the day will show it because it is to be revealed with fire, and the fire itself will test the quality of each man's work" (1 Cor. 3:13). However, this test is not speaking of purgatory fires in which Christians suffer but metaphorically of purifying fires of their works—Christians don't burn, worthless works burn! The wider context makes this clear. Paul is speaking of Christian works using the metaphor of a building (3:10). Every Christian worker builds on the foundation of the building—which is Jesus Christ" (3:11). Those who "add value" ("gold, silver, precious stones," 3:12) by building with lasting materials "will receive a reward" (3:14); those who use materials such as "wood, hay, straw"—materials that are not lasting and susceptible to combustion—will "suffer loss" (3:15). This is not the loss of salvation ("he himself will be saved," 3:15), but the loss of reward. The scene here is not purgatory but the judgment seat of Christ, of which Paul writes, "For we must all appear before the judgment seat of Christ, so that each one may be recompensed for his deeds in the body, according to what he has done, whether good or bad" (2 Cor. 5:10). When Paul adds the phrase "yet so as through fire," he is not saying that the Christian will be saved by *going through* the fire, but that he will be saved *from* the fire that will consume his works.

Some Catholic authors appeal to Hebrews 12:5–6, which says, "and you have forgotten the exhortation which is addressed to you as sons, 'My son, do not regard lightly the discipline of the Lord, / Nor faint when you are reproved by Him; / For those whom the Lord loves He disciplines, / And He scourges every son whom He receives.'" The argument of the Catholic here is that the terms "reproved" (Greek: *elenchomenos*) and "scourges" (Greek: *mastigoi*) are terms which indicate a suffering of Christians for sins they have committed after they have been justified. That suffering is for the purpose of paying the debt of that sin. Thus, it is claimed, Christ's death does not cover all sin and "Christ wills that we participate in his atoning work, at least with regard to discharging the debt of temporal punishment due for sin."[14] And if a Christian can suffer for his or her sins in this life, there is reason to think that, if such temporal suffering is insufficient, he or she will suffer in the next life—again, in order to purge the remaining sin.

This interpretation, however, fits neither the context of Hebrews 12, nor the teaching of the rest of the New Testament on the efficacy of Christ's cross work. First, the context of Hebrews is about the fatherly discipline for Christians; this is a discipline in love, for good, (Heb. 12:10) to sanctify them (in *this* life) and for "training" (12:11). The idea that this discipline, or reproof, or even scourging, is an atoning suffering that is meant to supplement the cross work of Christ (post-justification) must be imported into this context.

Second, the texts that do speak of the sufficiency of Christ's atoning work make it clear that "the blood of Jesus His Son cleanses us from *all* sin" (1 John 1:7). Titus 2:14 says that Christ "gave Himself for us to redeem us from every lawless deed, and to purify for Himself a people for His own possession, zealous for good deeds." This text indicates that Christians are

14 Karlo Broussard, *Purgatory is for Real* (El Cajon, CA: Catholic Answers Press, 2020), 45.

fully redeemed from "lawless deeds" and are being purified *in this life* for the doing of "good deeds" *in this life*. The process of sanctification in this life will not be extended to the next life.

The Christian has a hope in this life—a confident expectation—of seeing Jesus. And that expectation does not include purgatory. Here is how the apostle John expressed this hope: "Beloved, now we are children of God, and it has not appeared as yet what we will be. We know that when He appears, we will be like Him, because we will see Him just as He is. And everyone who has this hope fixed on Him purifies himself, just as He is pure" (1 John 3:2–3).

Another text to which Catholic writers appeal for support for the notion of purgatory is First Peter 1:7: "so that the proof of your faith, being more precious than gold which is perishable, even though tested by fire, may be found to result in praise and glory and honor at the revelation of Jesus Christ." Here the apostle Peter speaks of the Christian's faith being "tested with fire." Once again, this is not speaking of the fires of purgatory, but the metaphorical fires of persecution. The "fires" are not purging fires but proving fires—that reveal the genuineness of the Christian's faith in the face of "various trials" (1:6).

The Place of Purgatory in the Catholic Doctrine of Salvation

In order to appreciate the importance of purgatory in Catholic dogma one must understand the Catholic notions of "justification" and purification, as well as an understanding of the place of prayers for the dead and indulgences in the system.

The Catholic Idea of "Justification"

In the Roman Catholic theology of salvation, justification is a process that works along with sanctification. Justification is not (as in Reformed theology) a legal declaration, but must be a real cleansing from sin and will entail earning actual merit before God—a merit earned by the sinner himself or herself. If this is not accomplished in life, it must be after death. Thus for "Catholic theology, purgatory is necessary because it views salvation—and, hence, life with Christ in heaven after death"—as based on "not only the remission of sins, but also the sanctification and renewal of the interior man."[15]

15 Gregg R. Allison, *Roman Catholic Theology and Practice: An Evangelical Assessment* (Wheaton, IL: Crossway, 2014), 216; citing *Catechism of the Catholic Church*, paragraph 1989.

The Need for Final Purification

This process may, in some cases, be accomplished perfectly in this life; indeed, some rare individuals may earn more righteous merit than they need and that merit may be applied to others who meet certain conditions. If the process is not complete in this life (and assuming that the person is not still in a condition of mortal sin and unbelief) that person must undergo a process of further purification.

The Place of Prayers for the Dead and Indulgences

In the Catholic view of purgatory, prayers for the dead and indulgences play a key role. Catholics believe in a "mystical union" of all who are members of the body of Christ—the living and the dead. The living may, and should, pray for the dead.[16] Furthermore, "The Church also commends almsgiving, indulgences, and works of penance undertaken on behalf of the dead."[17] However, none of these practices can be supported from the canonical Scriptures.

Other Arguments Catholics make for the Dogma of Purgatory

- Belief in purgatory is an affirmation of belief in the immortality of the soul; it is ultimately a doctrine of hope.
- Belief in purgatory actually gives hope for those who die with little or no indication in life that he or she had made a life commitment or believed in Jesus Christ.
- Belief in purgatory gives a form of comfort to those whose faith is marginal; in these instances, those who have not been as faithful as they might have been on earth can expect that even though they will have to face the temporal torments of purgatory, they will not face the eternal torments of hell and will eventually be ushered into heaven.
- Belief in purgatory is a motive to live a more sanctified life; so a person is more attentive to attending Mass, performing works of mercy, and grace, penance, and other rites of the church.
- Belief in purgatory, praying for the dead, and making offerings for the dead, tends to make one more merciful and thoughtful to others.

---

16 Catechism of the Catholic Church, 300.

17 Catechism of the Catholic Church, 328.

BIBLICAL RESPONSE

In response to these other arguments it should be noted that the hope the New Testament speaks of is not mere "immortality" but a certain promise of being with Jesus (2 Cor. 5:8) and "paradise" with Jesus (Luke 23:43).

Also, the New Testament gives comfort and hope of eternal life only to those who—in this life—confess Christ (Rom. 10:9), abide in Christ (John 15), believe in Christ (John 20:31), are known by Christ (Matt. 7:15–23; John 10:14), and are one of His sheep who listen to His voice (10:27–28).

The motive to live a holy life, to serve others with works of mercy, is love for Christ. Christians are not taught to fear death and the afterlife, but to live in hope and with joy (Phil. 1:21) anticipating that death will usher them into the presence of the Lord (2 Cor. 5:8) or that they will be a part of the "blessed hope" (Titus 2:13), which is the rapture of the church (1 Thess. 4:13–18; 1 Cor. 15:50–57).

SUMMARY: THE PROTESTANT DENIAL OF PURGATORY

The Bible simply does not support the Catholic teaching of purgatory. As noted, the canonical texts to which Catholics appeal do not teach the doctrine of purgatory directly, nor can they be used to argue for it indirectly. Protestants do not accept the Apocrypha as an authority for doctrine on par with the canonical books; and yet, as noted, even the passage cited by Catholics from Second Maccabees 12 does not actually affirm the notion of purgatory.

Furthermore, Protestants deny the very rationale for purgatory. The Protestant doctrines of justification by faith alone and the imputation of Christ's righteousness make the very notion of purgatory untenable and unnecessary. It also follows that prayers for the dead and indulgences are effective for nothing, since all those who are "in Christ" when they die go to Him and have no need for further purification, since they are conformed to the image of Christ, justified, and glorified (Rom. 8:29–30). As First John 3:2 promises, "we will be like Him, because we will see Him just as He is."

Study Questions:

1. Where does the term "cemetery" come from and what does it mean? Why is it used for the place where people are buried?
2. What is the concept of "soul sleep"? Where did that concept originate and why?
3. What is purgatory? Where did that concept originate? What are some parallel concepts of purgatory?
4. Where does Roman Catholicism see purgatory in the church fathers?
5. Where does Roman Catholicism see purgatory in the Bible and the Apocrypha?
6. How does purgatory fit in the Roman Catholic doctrine of salvation?
7. What are the Protestant responses to the Roman Catholic doctrine of purgatory?

5

Common Questions About Life After Death

ANYONE WHO HAS OFTEN or regularly counseled the terminally ill or those who have lost loved ones knows that certain questions about death and the afterlife come up repeatedly. This chapter will attempt a preliminary biblical answer to some of these questions.

Do Loved Ones with Jesus See Us and Do They Know What Is Happening on Earth in Our Lives?

Many people like to think that a loved one who has died is "looking down" on them, with joy and approval, or in some way looking after them and still participating in their lives. It can be a comforting thought. However, there is nothing in the Bible that suggests that this is so. In a way that idea, while it may be in some way comforting to the living, does not consider the perspective of those who have gone on to be with the Lord. (For one thing, it must be admitted that some of what they would see, if they were "looking down" on their loved ones, would be distressing—and much of it frankly boring!)

The Bible indicates that heaven—the presence of the Lord—is a place of rest (Heb. 4:9 "So there remains a Sabbath rest for the people of God"; 4:11 "let us be diligent to enter that rest"). The apostle John writes in the book of Revelation, "And I heard a voice from heaven, saying, 'Write, "Blessed are the dead who die in the Lord from now on!"' 'Yes,' says the Spirit, 'so that they may rest from their labors, for their deeds follow with them'" (Rev. 14:13). The notion of "rest" here is not inactivity but of release from the burdens, worries, and concerns of temporal life and of the present evil age, and the freedom of joy and fellowship with the Lord and those who have preceded us in death. It should be a blessing for us to know that loved ones with Jesus are no longer distressed with the trials of life, the burdens of illness, the injustices of the wicked carried out on the righteous, and are at rest with their Lord.

Can Spiritualists or Mediums Contact the Dead? What Should We Think about Practices like Séances?

The Bible does mention such practices, but always in a negative light. In Leviticus 20:27 the LORD says bluntly, "Now a man or a woman who is a medium or a spiritist shall surely be put to death. They shall be stoned with stones, their bloodguiltiness is upon them." Likewise in Deuteronomy 18:9–11 Moses instructs Israel, as they were about to enter the promised land, "When you enter the land which the LORD your God gives you, you shall not learn to imitate the detestable things of those nations. There shall not be found among you anyone who makes his son or his daughter pass through the fire, one who uses divination, one who practices witchcraft, or one who interprets omens, or a sorcerer, or one who casts a spell, or a medium, or a spiritist, or one who calls up the dead." In the next verse (18:12) Moses says, "For whoever does these things is detestable to the LORD."

The New Testament also regards practices such as sorcery and other quasi-occult practices as unacceptable. In Acts 16, Luke records the apostle Paul's encounter with a young girl "having a spirit of divination. . . . Following after Paul and [his companions] she kept crying out, saying, 'These men are bond-servants of the Most High God, who are proclaiming to you the way of salvation'" (16:16–17). While a true statement, this was not the sort of testimony the apostle condoned, and being "greatly annoyed . . . he turned and said to the spirit, 'I command you in the name of Jesus Christ to come out of her!" (16:18). This put a stop to her demon-enabled powers of divination!

Luke also records (in Acts 8:9–24) the brief story of a man named Simon, who had practiced "magic arts" but was converted. When Simon saw the apostles bestow the Spirit by laying on of hands, he offered them money to be given this power (revealing that he still had some pagan notions from his former occupation). Peter rebuked him and called Simon's magic arts "wickedness" (8:22).

In First Samuel 28 there is the account of King Saul visiting a medium, a woman in the town of Endor (28:7). Saul wanted to speak to Samuel, who had died. Previously, Saul himself had outlawed the use of mediums (28:9), but he was so desperate for guidance that he disguised himself and went to the medium, asking her to "conjure up" Samuel (28:11). When Samuel actually did appear, the woman was surprised (probably because she was a fraud, a sham-medium; seeing an actual spirit appear was a shock!). Was this a real physical reappearance of Samuel, or merely an image of him? The text is not clear; regardless, Samuel indicates that this use of a medium was not appropriate—and this instance does not lend credibility to the practice of mediums and spiritualists.

This was another instance of Saul's sin and disqualification as king. After Saul's death First Chronicles 10:13–14 reveals that his death was a judgment, in part because he had consulted this medium: "So Saul died for his trespass which he committed against the LORD, because of the word of the LORD which he did not keep; and also because he asked counsel of a medium, making inquiry of it, and did not inquire of the LORD."

Jesus' parable of the rich man and Lazarus in Luke 16:18–31 would strongly suggest that once a person is dead, he cannot return to advise the living. As with the case of the young girl in Philippi (Acts 16:16–18), it seems that spiritists or mediums do not make contact with the spirits of deceased people, but with demons and "lying spirits" (1 Kings 22:23). All such practices—consulting mediums, joining séances, and so on—are clearly invalid and inappropriate for believers.

Are "Near-Death" Experiences, Accounts of "Trips to Heaven," or "Visitations from Heavenly Beings" Reliable Sources of What Happens after Death?

Most believers have heard accounts of so-called "near-death" experiences, where someone in a coma or even pronounced dead was revived. In some of these reports, the person recounts the experience, often in compelling detail. At times the person describes a bright light drawing them toward itself; of an emerging sense of peace; perhaps even a voice calling to them; only to be interrupted by the event of being physically revived.

Along the same lines, there are numerous accounts—many of them booklength—where a person has the opportunity (by some means) to take a tour of heaven, usually as the result of a "near-death" experience or a "vision." In a few cases the person recounting the "trip to heaven" claims an experience similar to that obliquely alluded to by the apostle Paul, which he describes as being "caught up to the third heaven" and "caught up to paradise" (2 Cor. 12:2, 4).

At times these "heavenly trips" are guided by "heavenly beings," or angels. Even if they do not take the person on a guided tour, the "heavenly visitor" is said to reveal information about heaven—information that the recipient finds comforting and reassuring.

What Is the Believer to Make of These Sources of Information about Heaven?

Simply put, these accounts are not reliable sources of information about heaven. They often claim to reveal aspects of heaven not confirmed by the Bible—even details that are incompatible with what the Bible does reveal about heaven, such as silly games, worldly diversions, and pleasures that have no place in the holy presence of God. These accounts often contradict one another—and themselves. The authors of these accounts seldom exhibit the humility and reticence to talk about such high and holy things, as Paul did (2 Cor. 12:4). These accounts are deliberately (and necessarily) vague and often repeat clichés about "bright lights," "pleasant-voiced guides," "heartfelt reunions with loved ones," and physical descriptions of heaven using the language of Scripture (e.g., Rev. 21–22), but often out of context, and in frankly mawkish ways. Not a few of these stories of "trips to heaven" have been thoroughly debunked.[1]

These accounts should not be given credibility. In John 3:13, the apostle affirms that "No one has ascended into heaven, but He who descended from heaven: the Son of Man"; that was true then, and there is no reason to think otherwise today.

There have been only a few prophets who were privileged to see a glimpse of the heavenly realm.

- Isaiah "saw the Lord sitting on a throne, lofty and exalted, with the train of His robe filling the temple" (Isa. 6:1). He recalls the wonder of the angelic chorus, the majesty and glory of the Lord, and his own unworthy sinfulness (6:2–5).
- Ezekiel, in the first chapter of his prophecy, records a vision of the Lord that was as weird and wonderful as it was magnificent and awe-inspiring. He finishes his record of the vision by saying, "Such was the appearance of the likeness of the glory of the Lord. And when I saw it, I fell on my face and heard a voice speaking" (Ezek. 1:28).
- The apostle John had a vision of the risen and glorified Christ (Rev. 1:12–16), and his response was to fall "at His feet like a dead man" (1:17).

1 See John MacArthur, *The Glory of Heaven: The Truth about Heaven, Angels and Eternal Life*, Second Edition (Wheaton, IL: Crossway, 2013), Chapter 1: "Heavenly Hash," 21–35.

None of these men, even in the inspired text of Scripture, speaks in the glib language of those who offer their accounts of their "trips to heaven," nor are they on such familiar terms with their "heavenly tour guides" (the angels). Paul even said of his elevation to the "third heaven . . . Paradise" (2 Cor. 12:2, 4) that he "heard inexpressible words" and that of such heavenly things "a man is not permitted to speak" (12:4). Paul also speaks of his experience in the third person, as an expression of humility and modesty.

In short, these inspired descriptions of visions of the LORD God in heaven, filled with majesty and awe, sound nothing like the trite and boastful stories about personal tours of heaven.

Study Questions:

1. What should believers say to those who think their deceased loved ones are "looking after them from heaven"?
2. What should believers say to those who think it is possible to contact their deceased loved ones through mediums and spiritists?
3. What should believers say to those who claim to have made a "trip to heaven and back" after a near-death experience?

6

Death and the Unbeliever

If death is an unpleasant subject to dwell on (as was noted in Chapter 1), death and the unbeliever is even harder to contemplate. For believers who have unbelieving loved ones and friends, the very thought of these dear ones suffering the loss of heaven and the pains of hell can be quite distressing, even heartbreaking. For the unbeliever, the biblical view of their prospects after death may be considered harsh, unloving, ungracious, and even repulsive. For these reasons it is all the more important to know what the Bible teaches about this subject. The question of what happens after death is too important to leave to personal opinion or popular and socially acceptable theories.

Four Certainties about Death and the Unbeliever

The Bible portrays the death of unbelievers in unambiguous and striking terms. There are at least four certainties concerning the death of unbelievers.

First Certainty: Death, for the unbeliever, is an unmitigated tragedy. At death, all that the unbeliever has lived for will end. As the Preacher of Ecclesiastes says, "there is no activity or planning or knowledge" in the grave (Eccles. 9:10). Proverbs 11:7 says, "When a wicked person dies, his expectation will perish, / And the hope of strong people perishes." Job concurs that those without God have no hope after death (Job 27:8). The Psalmist observes that at death the unbeliever's wealth and prestige are lost: "Even wise men die, / The stupid and the senseless alike perish / And leave their wealth to others. . . . But man in his pomp will not endure; / He is like the beasts that perish" (Ps. 49:10, 12). And the old adage "You can't take it with you" originated with the apostle Paul (1 Tim. 6:7).

The unbeliever's life is likened to a transient flower, or withering grass:

> Man, who is born of woman,
> Is short-lived and full of turmoil.
> Like a flower he comes forth and withers. (Job 14:1–2)

> All flesh is grass, and all its loveliness is like the flower of the field.
> The grass withers, the flower fades,
> When the breath of the LORD blows upon it;
> Surely the people are grass.
> The grass withers, the flower fades. (Isa. 40:6–8)

After this brief life the unbeliever's loss is total—described as "destruction" (Rom. 9:22; 2 Thess. 1:9; 2 Pet. 2:12). And Psalm 73:19 says, "They are destroyed in a moment! / They are utterly swept away by sudden terrors!"

This is why unbelievers live with the terror of death hanging over them. Job, in speaking of the death of the wicked, describes this.

> He lies down rich, but never again;
> He opens his eyes, and it is no longer.
> Terrors overtake him like a flood;
> A tempest steals him away in the night.
> The east wind carries him away, and he is gone,
> For it whirls him away from his place. (Job 27:19–21)

There is an inevitability and finality of death for the wicked. The Preacher of Ecclesiastes writes, "For the living know they will die; but the dead do not know anything, nor have they any longer a reward, for their memory is forgotten" (Eccles. 9:5). Second Samuel 14:14 poetically affirms this truth: "For we will surely die and are like water spilled on the ground which cannot be gathered up again."

Death will come to everyone; we have no control over it; we can't put it off. "No man has authority to restrain the wind with the wind, or authority over the day of death" (Eccles. 8:8).

Second Certainty: Death brings the unbeliever into a state of torment.

This is noted in the account of the rich man and Lazarus in Luke 16:23. Along the same lines, Job 26:5 says, "The departed spirits tremble." There will be the ultimate torment in hell (see Chapter 7), but no respite after death; the unbeliever will be subject to torments that anticipate his or her eternal judgment.

Third Certainty: Death initiates the unbeliever's eternal separation from God.

The eternal separation of unbelievers from God begins the moment they die and will continue forever. The apostle Paul states this: "These will pay the penalty of eternal destruction, away from the presence of the Lord and from the glory of His power" (2 Thess. 1:9).

Fourth Certainty: Death brings the unbeliever to God's judgment. Hebrews 9:27 makes this quite clear: "it is appointed for men to die once and after this comes judgment." And speaking of judgment, the author of Hebrews reminds his readers that God's judgment is terrifying (Heb. 10:27).

One commentator notes, "While death itself is a judgment that sinful man has brought upon himself [Ezek. 18:20a; Rom. 3:23], it is not the final judgment which, as something distinct, follows after death." That judgment will be "the final judgment after this life (Rev. 2:11; 20:6, 14f; 21:8)."[1]

It is appropriate to note here that the death of unbelievers brings no gratification to God. In Ezekiel 18:23 the prophet records a rhetorical question of the Lord: "'Do I have any pleasure in the death of the wicked,' declares the Lord God, 'rather than that he should turn from his ways and live?'" The expected answer is of course no, and later in the chapter it reaffirms this: "'For I have no pleasure in the death of anyone who dies,' declares the Lord God." His desires is for their repentance and life; so He invites all: "Therefore, repent and live" (18:32).

Alternative Views

Since the biblical view of death and the unbeliever is hard to think about for the believer and untenable (if not outright repugnant) to most unbelievers, it is not surprising that alternatives to, or adjustments of, the biblical view have been suggested. Three of these views will be discussed here.

Universalism

Universalism is the view that everyone—all people from all ages—will ultimately be saved. Some universalists hold that there is no hell and no punishment at all. Other universalists think that there may be some form of judgment (for some or all) but that no one will be sent to hell permanently. Some universalists deny that there is a hell (see Chapter 7).

Many universalists think that all religions lead to God and sincere belief in any religion is commendable before God. But even so, those who practice no religion will still be accepted into heaven.

---

1 Philip Edgcumbe Hughes, *A Commentary on the Epistle to the Hebrews* (Grand Rapids, MI: Eerdmans, 1977), 387.

Universalism has been advocated by various theologians throughout the course of the history of the Christian church. The early church fathers Clement of Alexandria, Origen, and Gregory of Nyssa taught a form of universalism. Origen even thought that Satan would ultimately be saved, and his views were declared heretical at the fifth ecumenical council—Constantinople II—in AD 553.

Some of those who hold this view take verses such as First Timothy 2:6 and First John 2:2 quite literally, explaining that Christ took away the sins of the "whole" world, such that there remains no basis for condemnation. Others simply assert that a God of love will save all his sentient creatures out of His compassion and benevolence.

This view is impossible to reconcile with the Bible's teaching that the unbelieving wicked will be condemned and eternally separated from God (as the Bible's teaching on hell makes clear).

Also, there are a number of verses that indicate that the salvation offered in the gospel of Jesus Christ and taught in biblical Christianity is an exclusive salvation. For instance, Acts 4:12 affirms, "there is salvation in no one else; for there is no other name under heaven that has been given among mankind by which we must be saved." The apostle Paul wrote, "there is one God, and one mediator also between God and mankind, the man Christ Jesus" (1 Tim. 2:5). And Jesus Himself said "I am the way, and the truth, and the life; no one comes to the Father but through Me" (John 14:6). Even the well-known text John 3:16, while it affirms "God so loved the world" also says that it is only those who believe in Him who will have eternal life; those who do not believe in Him will perish. John 3:18 makes this clear: "He who believes in Him is not judged; he who does not believe has been judged already, because he has not believed in the name of the only begotten Son of God." And in the same chapter John writes, "He who believes in the Son has eternal life; but he who does not obey the Son will not see life, but the wrath of God abides on him" (3:36).

Universalism is contradicted by the New Testament teaching that those who are saved are the elect (Matt. 24:31; Rom. 8:29–30; 2 Tim. 2:10, 19; Titus 1:1–3; 1 Pet. 1:1–3), are chosen before the beginning of the world (Eph. 1:3–12; Col 3:12; 1 Thess. 1:4–10; 2 Thess. 2:13–17; James 2:5), are predestined for salvation (1 Thess. 5:9; 1 Pet. 2:7–9), and are appointed to eternal life (Acts 13:48).

Inclusivism

Typically, when theologians use the terms inclusivism and its counterpart exclusivism, they are addressing the issue of who is saved and who is lost; that is, who will be in heaven and who will not be. Christian exclusivism restricts salvation and the promise of heaven to a limited group of people who have a special relationship with God by explicit personal faith and trust in the Person of Jesus Christ (that He is God and man—the incarnate Son of God) and the work of Christ (that He died on the cross for their sin).

Christian inclusivism is a view that must be differentiated from pluralism and universalism. Christian inclusivism, while affirming that the work of Jesus Christ is the only means of salvation, affirms that this salvation does not require personal and explicit knowledge of, or faith in, Jesus Christ in order for one to be saved.

Inclusivists typically affirm the truth of Acts 4:12, "And there is salvation in no one else; for there is no other name under heaven that has been given among mankind by which we must be saved." However, they point out, while this text indicates the necessity of Christ's work for salvation to happen, it does not speak of the necessity of the knowledge of that work.

The Rationale of Inclusivism: The Question of "Fairness"

Inclusivists argue that there is a basic unfairness to exclusivism. They reason that all those who lived before Christ had no opportunity to know or put their faith in Christ for salvation. In the same way, those who lived after Christ, in areas of the world where the gospel had not yet been preached, had no opportunity to know or put their faith in Christ for salvation. Furthermore, those who may have lived, or are still living, in countries where the gospel has been preached may still have had no opportunity to hear the true gospel or had the occasion to consider the message of the gospel carefully. The inclusivist argues that in the exclusivist view all these people, through no fault of their own, are unsaved and are therefore excluded from heaven. This is true even for those who have lived in places where they might have heard the message of Christ but did not believe for various and sundry reasons.

The inclusivist contends that if there was no opportunity to know the gospel, or that opportunity was never made sufficiently clear to a person (perhaps because someone was only exposed to false doctrines) it would be unjust for that person to be excluded from salvation and heaven. Inclusivists assert that God is not so unjust as to exclude those who never had an honest opportunity to put personal faith and trust in the Person and work of Jesus Christ. One advocate of this view writes, "inclusivism relieves us of those dark features of the tradition that suggest that (at worst) God plays favorites or (at best) inexplicably restricts his grace, so that whole groups are excluded from any possibility of salvation."[2] Inclusivists sometimes speak of "non-culpable" ignorance; that is, ignorance that is not due to a person's rejection of Christ, or his or her actual rebellion in sin. Such ignorance, they say, in fairness, God overlooks.

The Means of Inclusion

The question then becomes how (or in what way) the work of Jesus Christ is applied to those who do not have the opportunity or did not avail themselves of the opportunity to have knowledge of, or to put personal faith in, Jesus Christ. The answer to this question varies among inclusivists. For some inclusivists those who never hear of His name, or who never hear the gospel, may yet be given the gift of salvation and will be in heaven because they have an "instinct for God" that leads them to live up to God's universal moral standards, according to their God-given conscience. This is argued from Romans 2:14–15, where the apostle Paul writes about the "Gentiles who do not have the Law" but who nevertheless "instinctively perform the requirements of the Law." This "instinct" is an "instinct for God" and leads them to live as if they had the written Law of God. Paul explains: "these, though not having the Law, are a law to themselves, in that they show the work of the Law written in their hearts." It seems, argues the inclusivist, that the apostle is asserting that such people are living by a God-given internal (heart) impulse for moral living. Furthermore, "their conscience" is "testifying (that they are living rightly or wrongly before God) and their thoughts alternately accusing or else defending them," that is, their consciences are either convicting them of their moral failures or confirming to them that they are living rightly before God.

Along the same lines, some inclusivists suggest that the God-given revelation in nature, creation, and even within man himself has led many people to "seek God." Jeremiah 29:13 ("And you will seek Me and find Me when you search for Me with all your heart") promises that those who seek God sincerely will find God. The inclusivist suggests that God will be gracious

2 Clark H. Pinnock, "An Inclusivist View," in *Four Views on Salvation in a Pluralistic World*, ed. by Dennis L. Okholm and Timothy R. Phillips (Grand Rapids, MI: Zondervan, 1996), 101.

to those who see and respond to the "light of general revelation," and that He will accept the faith and reverence of those who live by that "light." So "Those also can attain to everlasting salvation who through no fault of their own do not know the gospel of Christ or His Church, yet sincerely seek God, and moved by grace, strive by their deeds to do His will as it is known to them by the dictates of their conscience."[3]

Inclusivists will cite the fact that Old Testament saints were saved before the message of the gospel of Jesus Christ and the preaching of the cross was made clear. David claimed this salvation, when he wrote in Psalm 37:39, "But the salvation of the righteous is from the Lord; / He is their strength in time of trouble." (See also 62:1, "My soul waits in silence for God only, / From Him is my salvation.") Hannah also claimed this salvation in her song of praise, "My heart exults in the Lord; / My horn is exalted in the Lord, / My mouth speaks boldly against my enemies, / Because I rejoice in Your salvation" (1 Sam. 2:1). Jonah affirmed, "Salvation is from the Lord" (Jonah 2:9), and he put no restrictions on how that salvation may be granted.

Inclusivists also cite the examples of Cornelius, a Roman centurion who was "a devout man and one who feared God" (Acts 10:1–2), and who was given the gift of the Holy Spirit (10:44) just as the apostles had on the day of Pentecost (11:15). This, an inclusivist will argue, shows that one who has not yet heard the gospel may be given the gift of salvation by the Spirit.[4]

Responses to the Inclusivist

On the Notion of the Justice of God

The inclusivist's appeals to the justice of God have a certain emotional appeal but ignore the biblical revelation of God's justice. God is just—but He is not obligated to act according to a human standard of what is or is not "just." Job 34:12 affirms, "Surely, God will not act wickedly, / And the Almighty will not pervert justice," yet Nahum 1:3 also affirms, "And the Lord will by no means leave the guilty unpunished." In God's view, no man has ever been just—save the Lord Jesus Christ Himself. God is not under any

3 Second Vatican Council, "Dogmatic Constitution on the Church, *Lumen gentium*, 21 November, 1964," in *Vatican Council II: The Conciliar and Post Conciliar Documents*, ed. Austin Flannery (Collegeville, MN: Liturgical Press, 1975), sec. 16.

4 See John Sanders, *No Other Name. An Investigation into the Destiny of the Unevangelized* (Eugene, OR: Wipf and Stock, 2001), 254; and Clark H. Pinnock, *Flame of Love: A Theology of the Holy Spirit* (Downers Grove, IL: InterVarsity Press, 1999), 203.

obligation to save anyone and every man's sin is worthy of the punishment God deems appropriate. It would be just for all to go to hell for all have sinned and fall short of the glory of God (Rom. 3:23); there is none righteous (3:10; see the complete indictment from the apostle Paul in 3:10–18). That any are saved at all is due to God's mercy and grace (9:22–23). When the entire picture of God's righteous sovereignty is seen in the light of human sin and depravity, the conclusion of the matter is to be found in Paul's words, "What shall we say then? There is no injustice with God, is there? May it never be!" (9:14).

On the Notion of Non-Culpable Ignorance

Even most human law systems do not allow that ignorance of the law is an excuse for violating the law. In the case of humans, the apostle Paul makes it clear in Romans 1 that the ignorance of men is self-imposed in that they suppress the truth in unrighteousness (1:18).

On the Notion of the Instinct for God

There is a "sense for God" (what John Calvin called the *sensus deiatus*[5]) but this is not the same concept as the inclusivist's "instinct for God." The Scriptural basis of Calvin's notion of the "sense," or "awareness" of God is in Romans 1. In Romans 1:20 Paul writes, "For since the creation of the world His invisible attributes, His eternal power and divine nature, have been clearly seen, being understood through what has been made." This is not a vague instinct, but a definite consciousness of God, "which is known about God" because it "is evident within them; for God made it evident to them" (1:19).

However, this does not, as the inclusivist's notion of the "instinct for God" suggests, lead men to submission and obedience to God, but having "suppress[ed] the truth in unrighteousness" (1:18) this knowledge of God ("even though they knew God," 1:21) is rejected, so men "did not honor Him as God or give thanks, but they became futile in their speculations, and their foolish heart was darkened. Professing to be wise, they became fools, and exchanged the glory of the incorruptible God for an image in the form of corruptible man and of birds and four-footed animals and crawling creatures" (1:21–23). This turn from God to idolatry leaves men "without excuse" (1:20) and subject to God's judgment (1:24, 26, 28—"God gave them over").

5 John Calvin, *Institutes of the Christian Religion*, ed. John McNeill (Louisville: Westminster John Knox Press, 2006), 44; the location in the *Institutes* is I. 3. 1.

On the Notion of Living by the Law

As noted previously, inclusivists sometimes appeal to Romans 2 and the apostle Paul's comments about Gentiles who do the things contained in the law (Rom. 1:14); from this they suggest that Paul is saying that the unbeliever who never hears the gospel can nevertheless be considered right with God because they live morally (as much as they can without the regenerating work of the Spirit). But here Paul is not suggesting that the Gentiles actually keep the law sufficiently to be saved, for Paul clearly says later in Romans 3:20, "by the deeds of the law no flesh will be justified in His sight." In Romans 2 Paul is contrasting the Jew—who claims to have the law (but is a lawbreaker) with the Gentile—who does not have the written law, but by his conduct shows that he knows right and wrong and sometimes does the right. "Gentiles do not always do what is right, but sometimes they do."[6] The point is the Jew is in no better a position before God then the Gentile—both are sometime law-keepers and sometime law-breakers; and all law-breakers as such are guilty before God.[7]

On the Notion of Seeking God

It may seem generally true that all (or at least many) men "seek God," especially when it is observed how pervasive religion (in various forms) seems to be in the many cultures and societies throughout history and even in the world today. Man seems to be *homo religiosus*. But on its own this inclination to religion and proclivity to worship does not constitute an acceptable "seeking," nor does it lead to true devotion to the true God. As noted previously, even the *sensus deiatus* which God has "made evident within them" leads men not to the true God, but to idolatry (Rom. 1:18–23). And Paul himself (in a later passage) says, "There is none who seeks for God" (3:1; Ps. 14:1–3). Men may be seekers of something—religious feelings, a vague spiritualty, religious experience (either to salve a wounded conscience or elevate one's longings for meaning in life, or to quell the terror of death), but such seekers are at the same time unrighteous before the Holy God, without understanding of the God of Truth, and have no genuine "fear of God" (Rom. 3:9–18).

---

6 Leon Morris, The Epistle to the Romans (Grand Rapids, MI: Eerdmans, 1988), 124.

7 The Gentile "knows enough of 'law' to be guilty when he sins, even though he may not know the God who prescribes right conduct." Morris, *Romans*, 125.

On the Light of General Revelation

The Bible does teach the fact and power of general revelation (Ps. 19:1–6). However, once again, this revelation does not "get through"[8] in such a way that men acknowledge and know God so as to obey and worship Him in truth. This is because, as noted previously, men "suppress the truth in unrighteousness" (Rom. 1:18). Paul elsewhere explains that "a natural man" that is one who is not a regenerated believer, "does not accept the things of the Spirit of God, for they are foolishness to him; and he cannot understand them, because they are spiritually appraised" (1 Cor. 2:14). That is, man on his own and with his sinful, God-rejecting mind, is unable to know the things of God from no matter what the source of revelation.

Paul describes the unbeliever in Ephesians 4 in stark terms. They live their lives "in the futility of their mind, being darkened in their understanding, excluded from the life of God because of the ignorance that is in them, because of the hardness of their heart; and they, having become callous, have given themselves over to sensuality for the practice of every kind of impurity with greediness" (Eph. 4:17–19). The expressions about the unbelievers' "futility of mind," their "darkened understanding," the "ignorance in them," and their "hardness of heart" all refer to what theologians call "the noetic effects of sin." The term "noetic" (from the Greek term *nous*, "mind") refers to the mind, or thinking (Greek *noein*, "to think") and the idea is that sin has had such a deleterious effect on man's thinking that apart from God's gracious work of illumination and the provision of the Spirit (1 Cor. 2:9–12) men will never "see" God's revelation in His creation, much less His Word. In sum, "Things which eye has not seen and ear has not heard, And which have not entered the heart of man, All that God has prepared for those who love Him. For to us God revealed them through the Spirit" (2:9–10).

On Salvation in the Old Testament

The inclusivist is right to believe that there were people saved in the Old Testament era and that the Old Testament saints lived in hope of going to heaven (or at least of entering the presence of God) after death. It does not

8 The very literal rendering of Psalm 19:3—"There is no speech, nor are there words; Their voice is not heard"—is understood by some to make the unexpected counterpoint to what the surrounding verses appear to be saying. In effect, the point is there is such a thing as general revelation in the heavens, but in effect, it is "not heard." The reason why this is so is explained in the main text above (see also Rom. 1:18; 1 Cor. 2:14).

follow, however, that this implies that there is a similar prospect of salvation or hope for individuals in all cultures and societies before Christ or in those after Christ that have never heard the gospel. The saints of the Old Testament would have put their faith in the person of the God of the Old Testament Who revealed Himself to them that they may know Him in truth. These Old Testament believers had His written Word (Gen. 15:6) and they would have looked forward in faith to the One who was the fulfillment of the types[9] of the Old Testament. Thus, when one looked in faith at the type (whether this was with full understanding or not) the Old Testament saint was trusting in God, in God's Word, and in the One (Christ) that would fulfill His Word.[10] Quite obviously this is not at all the case for cultures or individuals before or after Christ. Those without the Word (and who suppress the revelation in His creation, see previously) do not have the means to know God in truth. Jesus made it clear that faith in Him, in Him alone and in no other, is sufficient for salvation. In John 14:6, "Jesus said to him, 'I am the way, and the truth, and the life; no one comes to the Father but through Me.'"

On the Salvation of Cornelius

It may have been true that Cornelius was a saved man before the apostle Peter arrived at his house and preached Christ to him. But if that was the case, he would have been saved as were the Old Testament saints, that is, by faith in God's Word and the promises of the type-fulfilling Messiah to come. In that time, a Gentile who came to believe the God of the Old Testament and His word, but who did not submit to circumcision was called "a God-fearer" and this is how Cornelius was identified in Acts 10:2 "a devout man and one who feared God."[11] Again, the case of Cornelius cannot serve

9 A "type" (the Greek word *tupos* means "figure, model, or illustration") was a person, or place, or thing, or action (i.e., the Old Testament sacrifices, Heb. 9:19–26), or promise, or prophecy in the Old Testament that pointed to a fulfillment (an "anti-type") in the New Testament. The "anti-type" in many (if not most) cases is Jesus Christ.

10 *The Westminster Confession of Faith* (VI., 5) says, " . . . by promises, prophecies, sacrifices, circumcision, the paschal lamb, and other types of ordinances delivered to the people of the Jews, all fore-signifying Christ to come; which were, for that time, sufficient and efficacious, through the operation of the Spirit, to instruct and build up the elect in faith in the promised Messiah, by whom they had full remission of sins, and eternal salvation."

11 See Thomas R. Schreiner, "Proselyte," *The International Standard Bible Encyclopedia*, Vol. 3 (Grand Rapids, MI: Eerdmans, 1986), 1010.

to claim the possibility that those who have not heard the gospel of Jesus Christ may be given salvation for their devotion or reverence for God.

INCLUSIVISM IS NOT TENABLE

When examined critically in the light of what the Bible actually says, the arguments of the inclusivists are simply not compelling. Overall inclusivism falls short when examined in the light of what the Bible teaches about the need for one to know Jesus Christ, about the need to know what is revealed about Him and His work on the cross, about the need to put one's personal faith in Christ, and about the necessity to commit one's life to Him. Only then can one have the assurance of salvation and the hope of eternal life in heaven (John 20:31; Acts 2:36; Rom. 1:16; 10:8–13; 1 Cor. 1:18; 1 John 5:13).

ANNIHILATIONISM

The term "annihilationism" comes from the term "annihilate" which means "to destroy utterly," or "to obliterate something so as to cause it to cease to exist." The English term comes from the Latin *nihil*, "nothing." The doctrine of "annihilationism" has to do with the fate of some (or all) souls after death.

There are different types or views of annihilationism. Materialistic annihilationists believe that since all that exists is material, even human beings are just material beings—there is no immaterial part of human beings, that is, no soul or spirit. Therefore, at death human beings simply cease to exist; the body ceases to function, it decays, and the person simply is no more. The basis for this view is a materialistic worldview and is contradicted by the worldview of the Bible.[12]

12 Differences in beliefs that are based in wholly divergent worldviews cannot be debated on "neutral facts" and/or "objective data" because determining what constitutes a "fact" or is relevant as "data" will be determined by the divergent worldviews themselves. In this sense there are no truly "neutral" facts, nor is there genuinely "objective" data. The worldview of a materialist simply assumes that all claims to "facts," or "data," or any source of information about the afterlife (not to mention anything said about the afterlife in the Word of God) may be discounted because, well, there simply is no afterlife; this is virtually a presupposition of that worldview. The biblical worldview begins with the belief in the existence of God (Rom. 1:20; Heb. 11:1, 6); and along with that is belief in the self-revelation of God in His Word (John 17:17), the Bible. From these two basic presuppositions (and candidly, they are presuppositions) the believer can examine the "facts" about the afterlife that are revealed in that Word.

Another type of annihilationism, is called "conditional immortality" or "conditionalism." This view suggests all human beings are born naturally mortal, that is predisposed to die, and with that mortality the liability to cease to exist after death. In short, mortality, not immortality, is the default end for all human beings. Thus, unless one is given "eternal life" by God that person will (at some point[13]) cease to exist. It is only after God grants a believer "eternal life" that a person will one day experience "immortality."

Closely related to this view is what may be called "annihilationism proper." This view disagrees with conditionalism and teaches that all humans are created (born) with immortal souls, and that all would be immortal pending an action by God. That is, all humans would live on in the afterlife, either in hell (see Chapter 7) or in heaven, if God did not actively intervene. But God does actively intervene to limit the judgment of unbelievers and causes the annihilation of those souls who are in hell (as He has intervened to grant a believer the blessings of life in heaven). This is sometimes referred to as "terminal punishment."[14]

The distinction between (a) "conditional immortality" and (b) "annihilationism proper" turns on whether all human beings are (a) born naturally mortal and therefore believers must be given immortality to have "eternal life" and heaven or all human beings are (b) created (born) with immortal souls and unbelievers must have immortality taken away at some point.

Arguments of the Advocates of Conditional Immortality

Advocates of "conditional immortality" point out that the Bible teaches that human beings have been mortal ever since the Fall. Further they assert that in his fallen condition, man is incapable of living forever and doomed to die and cease to exist unless the Lord intervenes by giving him immortality. Several arguments from Scripture are put forward.

In Genesis 3:22–23 it is recorded that God expelled Adam and Eve from the garden in order that they would be prevented from taking "of the tree of life and eat[ing]" which if they did they would "live forever." It seems from

13 Some "conditionalists" see this removal of immortality at death (and therefore the annihilation comes at the moment of death). Other "conditionalists" see this removal of immortality after a (limited) time of punishment in hell or after the final judgment. The latter view is more common, and the following discussion will assume this view.

14 See John G. Stackhouse, "Terminal Punishment," in *Four Views On Hell*, Second edition, ed. by Preston M. Sprinkle (Grand Rapids, MI: Zondervan, 2016), 154ff.

this that without this provision they would not "live forever," and this must mean that they were not only physically mortal but were lacking immortality. In Revelation 22:2 access to the tree of life is restored—but only for the inhabitants of New Jerusalem. Immortality, it seems, is not the default condition of humans but the result of God's gift to those who believe.

Furthermore, it is argued, that God alone has immortality (1 Tim. 1:17; 6:16). Immortality, it is urged, is represented as a special gift connected with redemption in Jesus Christ (Rom. 2:7; 1 Cor. 15:53–54; 2 Tim. 1:10). Only God has "life in Himself" (John 5:26). Just so, life or eternal life is a gift from God (10:28; Rom. 6:22–23; Gal. 6:8).

Also, it is contended that immortality (and a new body in which to live immortally) are conditioned upon salvation. Paul's teaching in First Corinthians 15:50 and 53 speaks of that which is "perishable"—and here he is referring to believers and their perishable bodies. The believer, who is redeemed, in order to experience the full promise of salvation in the next life, "must put on the imperishable" that is, in the transition from this earthly existence to the full experience of heaven "this mortal must put on immortality." From this the advocates of conditional immortality argue that this is more than just the exchange of a "mortal body" for an "immortal body" but speaks of the need for God to specifically grant immortality to those who "inherit the kingdom of God." In short, "immortality" is conferred upon the believer but not the unbeliever.

Responses to the Advocates of Conditional Immortality

There are several biblical responses to the arguments of "conditional immortality." To begin with, it should be made clear that the advocates of "conditional immortality" have a mistaken understanding of "death." As noted previously, the basic biblical idea of death is separation. The advocates of "conditional immortality" seem to think of death and "mortality" as "ceasing to exist." However, when Adam sinned he died spiritually, but he did not cease to exist—he was separated from fellowship with God. When people die physically (as the result of Adam's sin, Rom. 5:12) their immaterial spirits are separated from their physical bodies. Human mortality, as such, refers to the mortal bodies of human beings, not to their immortal spirits or souls.

The notion that "immortality" must be granted to avoid the oblivion that comes at (or after) death is a misunderstanding and misapplication of the notion of "eternal life." The "eternal life" granted to believers is not "immortality" but a blessed condition of life that begins even before one dies, (John 3:36; 6:47). This "eternal life" once received will continue forever, even beyond one's physical death. In fact, Jesus defined "eternal life" in John 17:3 this way, "This is eternal life, that they may know You, the only true God, and Jesus Christ whom You have sent." In other words, "eternal life" is perpetual fellowship with God, through Jesus Christ. By contrast, "eternal death" is not a "ceasing to exist" but is a perpetual separation from God and is living forever without Christ.

The advocates of "conditional immortality" also have a mistaken understanding of the "tree of life" (Gen. 3:22–23). To begin with, it must be understood that this tree was (and will be, Rev. 22:2) a gracious provision for enjoying and sustaining those who are in right fellowship with God, and the life that the tree would (and will) sustain is appropriate only for those who are in right fellowship with God. It would not be a blessing to live a life sustained by the Tree of Life without a right relationship with God. Furthermore, it must be understood that the meaning of the expression "live forever" should be determined by the context. The Hebrew term *le'ōlām* ("forever") has the basic notion of "indefinite futurity," or "perpetuity" and it can also be used to express "everlastingness," or "endlessness." But again, only the context will determine which nuance is appropriate. In the context of Gen. 3:22, in reference to the Tree of Life, it seems best not to see the life that is promised as "unending—forever life" but as a "perpetual life to be lived without a right relationship with God." In other words, when God said that Adam "might stretch out his hand, and take also from the Tree of Life, and eat, and live forever," He did not mean man might eat of this Tree of Life and become somehow immortal[15] but that Adam may eat of this tree and then live perpetually for the rest of his life in his fallen state, in the conditions of judgment to which the Lord God had condemned him.

Finally, the new body that will be given to the believer at the resurrection (1 Cor. 15:50) is more than simply "imperishable," it will be glorious (see more on the resurrection body in Chapter 9). And the "immortality" the believer will experience is in contrast to the "mortality" and corruptibility of the natural human body. The "imperishable" and "immortal" bodies

15 This notion would be contradictory to the judgment from Genesis 2:17 ("in the day that you eat of it you shall surely die") that had already fallen on Adam. In other words, there is no thought that Adam might have avoided his judgmental death but eating from the Tree of Life. The idea that the Tree could, of itself, grant immortality is foreign to the entire account.

of believers are not in contrast to the "perishable" and "mortal" bodies of unbelievers, but to their own natural, pre-resurrected bodies. Paul in First Corinthians 15 is not suggesting the unbeliever will not be in some sense also resurrected in a body; the question of what sort of bodies the unbeliever will receive must be determined from the passages that speak of his or her judgement and punishment (see Chapter 7 on the conditions the unbeliever will face in hell).

Arguments of the Advocates of Annihilationism Proper

God and His Purposes

The advocates of "annihilationism proper" often have a different line of argument than do other annihilationists, often appealing to the nature of God and His purposes.

The most basic premise of "annihilationism proper" is that the idea of punishment of people in hell for eternity is inconsistent with God's love (1 John 1:5; 4:8, 16). The idea of eternal torment, even for heinous sins, and especially for the sins of most people (who are indeed sinners but are not notoriously evil like Ivan the Terrible or Adolf Hitler) is simply unjust and therefore inconceivable for the God who "so loved the world" (John 3:16). Annihilationists often cite the Scripture which says His anger endures for a moment, but his mercy endures forever (Ps. 103:8–14). Annihilationists usually are quick to affirm the holiness, righteousness, and justice of God as well as His love, benevolence, and goodness and that God is right and just to punish sin in hell.[16] Still, an annihilationist will argue that the sins of humans—even the sins of the worst sinners who ever lived on earth—are limited to one lifetime. They reason that it would be incommensurate for God to send His creatures into a place of eternal torment—unceasing punishment forever—for sins that lasted a finite number of years on earth.

Thus, annihilationists will grant that hell is real and the punishment is terrible, but they will also maintain that the punishment will eventually end. "Finite beings can perform only a finite amount of sin, and therefore a finite amount of suffering is sufficient to atone for it."[17]

---

16 The annihilationist's view of hell will be considered in the chapter devoted specifically to that topic.

17 Stackhouse, "Terminal Punishment," 78.

Unending Punishment is Inconsistent With God's Total Victory and Restoration of His Universe

Furthermore, to allow evil to exist—even under punishment, even in a place of darkness and separation from God and from all that is good—would mean that a part of His creation would be in eternal rebellion. It would, annihilationists argue, be an eternal blot of evil within His otherwise perfect and gloriously restored universe. It would amount to a defeat of God's intention for His creation, all of which was pronounced "very good" on the sixth day of creation (Gen. 1:31), for a bad place to exist eternally. A place of eternal torment of the eternally rebellious seems to be inconsistent with the declarations that Christ shall be over all (Eph. 1:10, 21–22) and that God shall be "all in all" (1 Cor. 15:28). The image of the culmination of God's purposes conveyed in Revelation 21:4 ("and He will wipe away every tear from their eyes; and there will no longer be any death; there will no longer be any mourning, or crying, or pain; the first things have passed away") is incommensurate with the image of a place of torment and despair that will exist forever. In short, it seems to the annihilationist that for hell to exist eternally would mean that in at least one dark corner of the universe God remains non-victorious.

The Meaning of "Eternal Punishment," "Destruction," and "Away from the Presence of the Lord"

The annihilationist admits the Bible teaches that the unbelieving wicked are "punished eternally" but they claim this is not to say that the wicked will undergo unending punishment. When the Bible says the unbeliever (the wicked, the lost) will suffer "eternal punishment" (Matt. 25:46), or "eternal judgment" (Heb. 6:2) or "eternal destruction" (2 Thess. 1:9), this means the same thing as the "eternal redemption" (Heb. 5:9; 9:12) of the believer. The believer is given the gift of immortality, which is a one-time happening, or experience that has eternal consequences. The believer is given the gift of eternal life once (1 John 5:11, 13), in this life before death, and that gift will last for eternity. This eternal life is not a process to experience but an outcome of a once-for-all-time event. Just so, the annihilationist argues, the unbelieving wicked are punished once, in hell, and in that punishment, they are "destroyed." It is not an eternal process of punishment or destruction.

The annihilationist argues that when Scripture speaks of the destruction of the unbelieving wicked the indication is that there is a single moment of utter, everlasting destruction—an annihilation. It is a moment in time with lasting results. Psalm 73:19 says, "How they are destroyed in a moment! They are utterly swept away by sudden terrors!" Psalm 92:7 says "when the wicked sprouted up like grass / And all who did iniquity flourished, / It was only that they might be destroyed forevermore." The annihilationist argues that the wicked are destroyed forever, but they are not forever being destroyed. In Second Thessalonians 1:8–9, the apostle Paul says the Lord Jesus will bring "retribution to those who do not know God and to those who do not obey the gospel of our Lord Jesus. These will pay the penalty of eternal destruction, away from the presence of the Lord and from the glory of His power." The annihilationist argues that "away from the presence of the Lord" must mean annihilation because an omnipresent God would still be "present" to those in hell. In any case, the annihilationist suggests annihilation fits the apostle's language as well or better than eternal conscious punishment.

Examples and Metaphors of God's Punishment

Old Testament

The annihilationist argues that there are Old Testament instances which seem to indicate that God's judgment of the wicked is terminal, that is, it is a one-time event with (ever)lasting consequences. The apostle Peter describes the judgment on Sodom and Gomorrah (Gen. 19:29) as a "destruction" that reduced "them to ashes" (2 Pet. 2:6). For anyone who failed to live under the covenant-Law God had given the people, the LORD promised to "blot out his name from under heaven" (Deut. 29:20). This judgment would be like the destruction of Sodom and Gomorrah "which the LORD overthrew in His anger and in His wrath" (29:23).

Isaiah describes the destruction of the unbelieving wicked with the image of fire that consumes as dry grass and stubble are burned up, "as a tongue of fire consumes stubble / And dry grass collapses into the flame, / So their root will become like rot and their blossom blow away as dust" (Isa. 5:24). The image here, the annihilationist says, is a complete destruction.

The annihilationist suggests that many texts in the Psalms speak of the judgment of the unbelieving wicked in terms that seem to indicate a terminal judgment. In Psalm 37 David says, "For evildoers will be cut off, / But those who wait for the LORD, they will inherit the land" (37:9). David further describes this judgment in these terms: "But the wicked will perish; / And the enemies of the Lord will be like the glory of the pastures, / They vanish—like smoke they vanish away" (37:20); "But transgressors will be altogether destroyed" (Ps. 37:38). These terms, claims the annihilationist, describe a disintegration into nothingness.

New Testament

Like the metaphor of fire used by Isaiah above, the annihilationist points to a number of instances in the New Testament where fire is used to describe the destruction of the unbelieving (Matt. 3:10; 7:19; 13:40; John 15:6)—and this is seen to indicate a complete burning up, an utter consuming judgment (Heb. 6:8; 10:27; Jude 7; Isa. 33:11).

In one well-known instance, Jesus told His disciples, "Do not fear those who kill the body but are unable to kill the soul; but rather fear Him who is able to destroy both soul and body in hell" (Matt. 10:28). This seems to suggest that just as a body may be destroyed (i.e., cease to exist), so in hell souls will be destroyed (i.e., cease to exist). It appears that Jesus is saying the souls of the unbelieving will not go on existing in a conscious state in hell after it has been destroyed.

Responses to the Advocates of Annihilationism Proper

As not a few theologians and Christian believers have admitted, the idea of "terminal punishment" is compelling, just because the idea of eternal torment seems so repugnant to any caring and compassionate human being. Even so, this apparently reasonable opinion is flawed. It is an emotionally driven, human viewpoint, and not based on a straightforward and reasonable assessment of the revelation in the Bible concerning the destiny of unbelievers. In short, the human perspective is not the divine perspective—especially when it comes to judgment and fairness. God is all-loving, compassionate, and benevolent, perfect in holiness, justice, and righteousness. The annihilationist simply does not stand in the place where God stands—in eternal, absolutely just, perfect righteousness and transcendent holiness—so he is in no position to say it would be incommensurate for God to send any of His creatures into a place of torment forever. If the transcendently holy and perfectly just God of all creation deems it appropriate to send sinners to an eternal hell, who can say He is not just? The "Judge of all the earth" will "deal justly" (Gen. 18:25). It is not the annihilationist's, nor any human being's, sense of fairness, justice, compassion, or righteousness that must answer the question of divine justice. The only viewpoint or perspective that matters is found in what God has revealed about Himself—His standard of righteousness, and what He deems to be the appropriate punishment for those who are not believers in Jesus Christ and recipients of His grace. The annihilationist admits that God is just to punish sin, but it is also true that all sin is against an infinitely holy God and that He alone can determine the extent and duration of sin's punishment.[18]

Another annihilationist argument is that the existence of a place of eternal torment would deny God a complete victory over His foes—that the anticipated restoration of all things would be unfinished forever. This, however, misses a key point about God's creation in the first place—that God created everything for His glory. Since God created all things for His glory (Rev. 4:11; 1 Chron. 29:11) that means all things exist to manifest or display His glory (Ps. 19:1). He made all things to reveal that He alone is God (Isa. 45:18). Just as heaven will manifest and display His attributes of grace, mercy, love, and benevolence eternally, so hell will manifest and display His attributes of perfect justice and righteousness—His hatred of sin, His victory over Satan and all evil—for eternity.

A related principle can be seen in the truth that God is glorified in the judgments He brings on His enemies. In Isaiah 66 the prophet speaks of such a judgment:

> But He will be indignant toward His enemies.
> For behold, the Lord will come in fire,
> And His chariots like the whirlwind,
> To render His anger with fury,
> And His rebuke with flames of fire.
> For the Lord will execute judgment by fire,
> And by His sword on all flesh,
> And those slain by the Lord will be many. (66:14–16)

Then the prophet records the words of the Lord Himself, in which He explains this judgment: "For I know their works and their thoughts; the time is coming to gather all nations and tongues. And they shall come and see My glory" (66:18). Isaiah is revealing here that God's judgments on earth in history display His glory. Just so, from this it can be concluded the eternal judgment of the unbelieving wicked is intended to eternally display His glory.

---

18 The fact that Christ's death was for sinners (that is, for those who put their faith in Him), was that of an infinitely holy sacrifice, of infinite value, for sins against an infinitely holy God, may be taken as an indication of what is the appropriate punishment of sinners who do not trust in His death for the payment of their sins.

The annihilationist also argues that hell would thwart God's plan to restore all things to Himself. But this is a misunderstanding of the goal of God's plan and of the meaning of "restore." The anticipated restoration of all things is not to make every part of His creation pristine and exactly as it was at the end of creation week (Gen. 1:31)—i.e. "very good." That description referred to the world that had been created by God for human habitation. At that point the world was "very good" in its potential for humans to live on the earth, to serve God and to have a relationship with God that would abound to the glory of God. It was very good for that purpose, and yet it still needed to be cultivated and kept (to use the terms of Gen. 2:15). The "restoration" to come will be a restoration to that purpose—again, the glory of God.

Furthermore, there was the development and outworking of God's plan for this "very good" creation (Eph. 1:11; 3:11). In that plan there were developments—in history, in the lives of believers, etc.—that seemed to threaten or derail that plan (e.g. mankind's sin in the era of Noah; the Tower of Babel; all the enemies of the nation Israel) but not one of these threats permanently thwarted or long disrupted God's plan. He overcame the threats and He continued the outworking of that plan; and He will continue that outworking until the plan is finished. The culmination of that eternal purpose is the ultimate goal; and that goal is, once more, the glory of God. In short, the purpose of God is for His glory, not to make everything "very good" or restore the world to suit human beings. He will "restore" all things by bringing them to their original purpose which is to glorify Him!

What is the meaning of "the restoration of all things?" In Acts 3:21 Peter refers to "the period of restoration of all things about which God spoke by the mouth of His holy prophets from ancient time." This is the millennial kingdom[19] when the nation of Israel and the nations of the earth will live under the rule of "KING OF KINGS, AND LORD OF LORDS" (Rev. 19:16). The nations will be brought into alignment with each other and under the hegemony of the Lord Jesus Christ. This is the "restoration" Peter spoke of and this is the type of "restoration" which will happen when God's purposes are realized in the eternal state—that is, everything will be in proper relationship to, restored to its rightful place, before the Sovereign God. The wicked and unrepentant unbelievers will be under His eternal punishment and the redeemed believers will enjoy His glory.

19 "The period of the restoration of all things is another name for the future earthly reign of Christ, the millennial kingdom." John MacArthur, *Acts 1–12: The MacArthur New Testament Commentary* (Chicago, IL: Moody Publishers, 1994), 121.

The annihilationist argument that "eternal punishment" means "a one-time punishment that has lasting effects (that is, the punished cease to exist forever) falters when it is pointed out that this understanding of "eternal" does not work for the "eternal life" of the believer. As noted previously, "eternal life" is not a one-time gift with lasting effects, but a quality of life that begins in this life and will continue forever (John 3:36; 6:37). Furthermore, the descriptions of hell (which will be described in Chapter 7) do not accord with the idea that the punishment of the unbeliever will end.

Similarly, the annihilationist's appeals to the terminology of "destruction," or to the Old Testament examples of judgment (such as Sodom and Gomorrah), or to the terminology of the consuming nature of fire, are irrelevant because they do not themselves prove that God's judgment is always a "one time event with eternal terminal results." These instances do speak of a terminal destruction in the temporal sphere (that is, there is a destruction, or consuming, with reference to this life) but to determine the duration and extent of God's judgment in the next life, appeal must be made to texts that actually refer to that judgment. The texts that directly refer to the judgments of hell describe hell as "eternal fire" (Matt. 25:41; Jude 1:7), "unquenchable fire" (Mark 9:43), "eternal punishment" (Matt. 25:46), where "worm does not die, and the fire is not quenched" (Mark 9:48; Isa. 66:24), "the penalty of eternal destruction" (2 Thess. 1:9), where "the smoke of their torment goes up forever and ever; they have no rest day and night" (Rev. 14:11), where "black darkness has been reserved forever" (Jude 1:13). These texts do not indicate a one-time destruction with eternal results but an ongoing experience that lasts for eternity—which we will discuss in the next chapter.

Study Questions:

1. What are the four certainties about death and the unbeliever?
2. What is the basic idea of universalism and why is it untenable?
3. What is the basic idea of inclusivism? What is the rationale of inclusivism?
4. What are the means of salvation that inclusivism appeals to (for those who do not hear the gospel)?
5. What are the biblical instances that inclusivism appeals to argue that its rationale is tenable?
6. Why is inclusivism untenable?
7. What is the basic idea of annihilationism? What are the types of annihilationism?
8. What is "conditional immortality" or "conditionalism"?
9. What are the responses to "conditional immortality" from the Bible?
10. What is annihilationism proper? What are the arguments of annihilationism proper?
11. What are the Old and New Testament examples to which annihilationists appeal to in support of annihilationism?
12. What are the counterarguments to annihilationism proper?

7

Hell

HELL, LIKE DEATH, MAY not be a pleasant topic to discuss, but we need to discuss it, because it is clearly a biblical doctrine, and we should have a clear understanding of it.

The Arguments of those who deny a Literal Hell

Before we delve into what Scripture has to say about this doctrine, let's look at the arguments of those who deny a literal hell.

"Hell is a myth."

Many of those who reject the idea of hell do so because they think it is a myth, a relic of pre-scientific thinking. They suppose that it is the remnant of a bygone age when men and women believed that the forces of nature and the events of life were controlled by the gods who were angry with human beings and who would act in a vengeful or malicious way if offended. Not a few others think that the doctrine of hell harkens back to the theology of the Medieval era when the church used the threat of the terrors of hell to keep the people fearful and thus dependent on the rites and sacraments of the church. Now, they say, scientifically minded people know better and regard the terrors of hell as no different than the myths of ancient cultures.

This is the materialist's view of hell—it is a myth, it does not exist. This view is not as much a rejection of hell as it is a so-called logical conclusion, or at least a reasonable assumption, based on a worldview that rejects the God of the Bible and the truthfulness and authority of the Bible. In other words, the issue with such folks is not hell itself, but the God revealed in the Bible (which itself is a book that they reject)—such a God, they believe, does not exist.

"Hell is now."

For not a few people, the idea of hell is not eschatological, but a present reality; in other words, it is not something that looms in the murky "undiscovered country"[1] of the afterlife. Hell is the environment that man makes for himself and others on earth.

As proof, they point to such social ills as the injustices of totalitarianism, the scourge of poverty, rampant environmental destruction, the Holocaust, genocide, and world wars. Even a life of pursuing wealth, fame, and power, they say, can be something of a hell—a tortured chase after selfish desires at the expense of enjoying life—whether or not that pursuit is successful.

There is some truth to these ideas; life can be "hellish" for some people. And yet, while it is true that life in this post-Genesis 3 world (i.e. fallen and populated with sinners) can be "hellish" at times, such a view is shortsighted. Such a dismal assessment of life here and now does not take the Bible any more seriously than the "hell is a myth" theory. So once again, this is a rejection, not of a literal hell, but of the God of the Bible (and addressing the rejection of God goes well beyond the scope of this book).[2]

"Hell is a metaphor or symbolic."

In some ostensibly Christian theologies (at the liberal end of the spectrum), the Bible's many references to hell are taken to be metaphorical, symbolic and/or indicative of how much God hates sin, or how destructive sin is for human beings. The language of a hell as "fire and brimstone" (Ps. 11:6; Rev. 20:10) is to be understood as symbolic of the terrors of final punishment, but not "literal" in the sense that anyone would actually be sent to such a place.

---

1 This description of what comes after death is found in Shakespeare's play *Hamlet*, Act 3, Scene 1 (in the famous "to be or nor to be" soliloquy).

2 See Cornelius Van Til, *Why I Believe in God* (Philadelphia, PA: Westminster Theological Seminary, 1976); and Greg Bahnsen, *Always Ready: Directions for Defending the Faith* (Nacogdoches, TX: Covenant Media Press, 1996). These authors do not try to prove the existence of God (they contend that his existence is an axiom that must be presupposed); they seek only to demonstrate how questions such as the existence of God, the truthfulness and authority of the Bible, and, indeed, the question of the reality of hell, are determined by one's worldview. In short, for those who know that God exists ("anyone who comes to him [God] must believe that he exists," Heb. 11:6,NIV) and know that His Word is truth (John 17:17), there is no question that hell exists. On the other hand, those who begin with a worldview that denies or ignores these facts ("The fool has said in his heart, 'There is no God,'" Ps. 14:1) will never be convinced of the reality of hell, until (very sadly) they experience it for themselves, or are converted to the true worldview of Scripture. That conversion happens when the Spirit of God uses the Word of God preached (Rom. 10:17) and the gospel (see Appendix A) to cause someone to be born again (1 Pet. 1:3–9).

"God is too loving to send people to hell."

Modernist theologians (and many non-theologians as well) believe in a God who is "too loving and forgiving" to send people to hell. In many cases, these folks think society has moved beyond thinking God is vengeful and think of Him only as a loving God; for such a God, hell would have no purpose, for God's dealings with mankind are always benevolent.

SUMMARY OF DENIALS OF HELL

This brief survey of arguments for the rejection the biblical doctrine of hell is only a sampling of the rationalizations in many books, articles, and blog-posts that dispute, or flatly deny, the reality of hell. To deal with every variant of these arguments would be impossible; to cover all the major ones would be beyond the scope of this book; even to deal with a few in detail would detract from the purpose of this book.[3] A better way to proceed is to articulate the biblical view—which is that hell is real.

THE BIBLICAL DOCTRINE OF HELL
SPECIFIC TERMS AND EXPRESSIONS FOR HELL

Gehenna

The term *gehenna* is the Greek transliteration of an Aramaic term, *gēhinnām*, which in turn is from the Hebrew *gê hinnōm* ("Valley of Hinnom" or "valley of the sons of Hinnom," 2 Kings 23:10; 2 Chron. 28:3). This valley is to the southwest of Jerusalem and at one point joins with the Kidron Valley on the south and east of Jerusalem. This was the site of "Topheth" (Isa. 30:33; Jer. 7:31), a place of Baal worship, where the detestable and horrific practice of child sacrifice to the god Molech took place (2 Kings 16:3; 21:6; 23:10; 2 Chron. 28:3; 33:6; Jer. 7:31; 19:2–6). In this place, children were burned to death, i.e., made to "pass through the fire" (2 Kings 16:3; 21:6; 23:10; 2 Chron. 33:6). Other texts which refer to this are "burned his sons in fire," (28:3); "to burn their sons and their daughters in the fire" (Jer. 7:31); and "to burn their sons in the fire as burnt offerings to Baal" (19:5). Jeremiah prophesied that this site would

3 For those interested, a fairly recent book of scholarly articles by a few of the best evangelical biblical scholars that answers many of the more recent denials of the biblical doctrine of hell is Christopher W. Morgan and Robert A. Peterson, eds., *Hell Under Fire: Modern Scholarship Reinvents Eternal Punishment* (Grand Rapids, MI: Zondervan, 2007).

become a place of future judgment, calling it "the valley of Slaughter" (Jer. 19:6). The site was so infamous that in later years, after the Babylonian captivity, it became the city's dump site for the bodies of criminals, animal carcasses, and rotting garbage. The accumulated refuse would often spontaneously burn, or fires would be set to consume corpses. These fires would create an acrid, horrible-smelling, sickening smoke. Inevitably the location came to be called the "valley of fire." Virgil Cruz comments, "Because of such associations, by the first century B.C., gehenna came to be used metaphorically for the hell of fire, the place of everlasting punishment for the wicked. This understanding is discernible in Jewish apocalyptic literature (e.g., 2 Esdr. 7:36)."[4]

The term *gehenna* occurs twelve times in the New Testament, eleven of which are in the Gospels; seven in Matthew (Matt. 5:22, 29, 30; 10:28; 18:9; 23:15, 33; three in Mark 9:43, 45, 47; once in Luke 12:5; once in James 3:6). Jesus used the term *gehenna* to refer to the place of ultimate, fiery punishment—that is, hell.

Lake of Fire

The "lake of fire" is an expression that appears in only a few places in the book of Revelation (Rev. 19:20; 20:10, 14, 15; 21:8). The description of the lake of fire as a place of "fire which burns with brimstone" (19:20; 20:10; 21:8), and a place of torment "where the beast and the false prophet . . . will be tormented day and night forever and ever" (20:10), and the place of the second death (20:14, "This is the second death, the lake of fire"; 21:8), and the final destination of those whose names were "not found written in the book of life" (20:15) makes it unmistakable that this is another name for hell—perhaps the primary name for hell.

Hell Is Distinguished from Hades

The Greek term *hadēs* was used in Greek mythology for both the god of the underworld and the abode of the dead. As noted in Chapter 3 (under the heading "The Mystery of the Intermediate State/*Hades*"), hades is the term used in the ancient Greek version of the Old Testament (LXX) for Sheol (see Chapter 3, under the heading "The Mystery of the Intermediate State/*Sheol*"). In common usage today the term "hades" it is often interchangeable with the term "hell." However, it seems better to view hades as something like "an underground

4 Virgil Cruz, "Gehenna," in *Evangelical Dictionary of Theology*, 2nd edition, ed. Walter A. Elwell (Grand Rapids, MI: Baker, 2001), 480.

prison with locked gates to which Christ holds the key" (Matt. 16:18; Luke 16:23; Acts 2:27, 31[5]).[6] As such, it appears that hades "is a temporary place that will give up its dead at the general resurrection."[7] Also Rev. 20:14 says that after the final judgment, "Then death and Hades were thrown into the lake of fire." Since the lake of fire is another name for hell (see above) it seems that hades—which will be thrown into hell—is something that has served its purpose and will be dispensed with. It is clearly distinct from hell itself.

THE BIBLICAL PICTURE OF HELL

Hell Is a Literal Place

Jesus and others in the New Testament described hell as a real place to which people are consigned by God's judgment. There are some who prefer to think of hell as a "condition" that a person brings on himself or herself. Pope John Paul II expressed this view in 1999 when he said, "Hell is not a punishment imposed externally by God, but the condition resulting from attitudes and actions which people adopt in this life."[8] But that can hardly fit with the biblical language that speaks of those who will be thrown "into the furnace of fire; *in that place* there will be weeping and gnashing of teeth" (Matt. 13:42; 25:30). The language of Rev. 20:15 ("And if anyone's name was not found written in the book of life, he was thrown into the lake of fire") refers to a place into which the unbeliever is cast or tossed.

Hell Is a Place of Darkness

Jesus Himself called this the place of "outer darkness" (Matt. 25:30); the apostle Peter and Jude called it "black darkness" (2 Pet. 2:17; Jude 1:13);

---

5 In Acts 2:27 Peter, quoting Psalm 16, says "the Holy One" (namely Jesus) would not be abandoned to hades. It is best to understand that Jesus was kept out of hades altogether, than to think He went to hades and was rescued out of hades. Jesus told the thief on the cross that on that very day He and the thief would be in Paradise, that is, heaven (Luke 23:43). Jesus never went to hell or to hades after His death on the cross.

6 William D. Mounce, ed., *Mounce's Complete Expository Dictionary of Old and New Testament Words* (Grand Rapids, MI: Zondervan, 2006), "Hades," 316.

7 Mounce, 316.

8 Pope John Paul II, "General Audience," Wednesday, July 28, 1999, released by the Vatican News Service; https://www.vatican.va/content/john-paul-ii/en/audiences/1999/documents/hf_jp-ii_aud_28071999.html accessed September 9, 2022.

or (in some translations) "gloom of darkness." The expression in Second Peter and Jude is *zophos tou skotos*, and does not simply mean a dimness or even dismal darkness. The term *zophos* is a much more expressive term and refers to the gloomy, depressing—even hopeless—darkness associated with the nether world, that is, hell. This is a darkness that is so impenetrable and oppressive that it can (metaphorically) be sensed or felt.

In the Bible "light" describes God: "God is Light" (1 John 1:5); Jesus is "the Light of the world" (John 8:12); fellowship with God happens in the light (1 John 1:7). Light is the realm of the children of God (Eph. 5:8; 1 Thess. 5:5) and in the light are "goodness and righteousness and truth" (Eph. 5:9). Thus, as a place of darkness, hell is the absence of God's benevolent presence, a place of no fellowship with God, a place for those who are *not* children of God; hell is a place where its residents are devoid of "goodness and righteousness and truth."

Hell is a Place of Anguish and Torment

The expressions used to describe the experience of those in hell provide graphic confirmation that it is a place of anguish, pain, and torment. In Matthew 13, Jesus tells a parable about two kinds of seed—good seed and tares. "The good seed, these are the sons of the kingdom; and the tares are the sons of the evil one" (Matt. 13:38). At the end of this parable—after the part about the tares being "gathered up and burned with fire" (13:40)—Jesus makes this application: "So shall it be at the end of the age. The Son of Man will send forth His angels, and they will gather out of His kingdom all stumbling blocks, and those who commit lawlessness, and will throw them into the furnace of fire; in that place there will be weeping and gnashing of teeth" (13:40–42). This expression indicates that hell will be a place of sorrow and grief ("weeping") and of deep distress; the "gnashing of teeth" (literally, the "grinding of teeth") indicates a person in excruciating pain. Hell will be a place of torment (Rev. 20:10), and will entail both intense physical suffering and severe mental anguish.

In Mark 9, where Jesus is warning his disciples to avoid hell (Mark 9:38–48), He describes hell as the place "where the worm does not die." This quotation of Isaiah 66:24 is one of the most graphic and horrifying images of hell in the Bible. The picture of one's own decaying body covered with loathsome worms is indeed ghastly! The use of the personal adjective "their" seems to suggest that the condemned person has his or her own personal worm feeding on them, and that this devouring will continue constantly and unceasingly, for this worm does not die! The worst aspect of the image is that the person who is subjected to this appalling circumstance will be fully aware of it and consciously experience it! It is not necessary to suggest that the image be taken so literally as to affirm actual immortal worms feeding on eternally decaying flesh. Jesus' image is of a horrific experience for those in hell; it is a place of unimaginable misery and anguish.

Hell is a Place of Fire

As just noted above, hell will be a place of fire; the unbeliever will, like the tares in the Matthew 13 parable, be thrown "into the furnace of fire" (13:50). Jesus spoke of hell as "eternal fire" on several occasions (5:22; 18:8–9; 25:41). In Mark 9:43 and 48, Jesus describes the fire as "unquenchable"—that is, unending, incapable of being extinguished or burning itself out.

Those who object to the notion of a literal fire may be missing the point. It may simply be beyond the finite capacity of human beings limited to the temporal and earthly perspective to explain how a fire can be a "real fire" and yet an "eternal fire." However, the truth that must be affirmed, given the many references to fire in the Bible's description of hell, is that whatever "is real" in this punishment of the unbelieving wicked will be eternal, and it will be as painful and excruciating for the sufferer in eternity as "real fire" would be in this temporal realm. In short, it seems best to affirm that there is "an eternal fiery" punishment in hell, despite the conceptual difficulties of a "real eternal fire." It has been said, that if hell is *not* a "real eternal fire" it is surely something worse.

Hell is a Place of No Repentance

In the parable of the talents in Matthew 25, Jesus describes the fate of the "wicked, lazy slave" (25:26; also described as a "worthless slave," 25:30). Because of his faithlessness and unbelief, his master commanded that he be thrown "into the outer darkness; in that place there will be weeping and gnashing of teeth" (25:30; 8:12). As noted, this place of "outer darkness" is hell and the fact that those in hell are "weeping" expresses the sorrow and grief felt by those who find themselves there. This is not a sign of repentance toward God but an expression of self-pity. There is no indication that those in hell—even then!—feel remorse or a desire to submit to the lordship and sovereignty of God. They will not—even then!—ask for His forgiveness.

As noted, this expression "gnashing of teeth" (25:30) depicts the intense pain felt by those in hell. However, this expression appears in several other contexts such as in Psalm 37:12. Here David describes the wicked man as one who "plots against the righteous, / And gnashes at him with his teeth." Likewise, in Psalm 35 the psalmist speaks of "malicious" (35:11) persons who afflict and slander the humble, righteous man. The psalmist says they are "Like godless jesters at a feast" and adds, "They gnashed at me with their teeth" (35:16). In these instances the "gnashing of teeth" is a gesture of offense directed at another. In Psalm 112 the psalmist says that when the wicked man sees the prosperity and generosity of the righteous, he will "be vexed" and he "will gnash his teeth and melt away" (112:10), that is, he will be angry and resentful. Here again is evidence that those in hell will not be repentant, but will "gnash their teeth" at God, that is they will be making a gesture that indicates they still do not honor God, but are angry and resentful. This is another indication that those in hell are still rebellious and bitter toward God.

Again, another indication that there is no repentance in hell can be seen in the parable of the rich man and Lazarus (Luke 16:19–31), considered in an earlier chapter. The attitude of the rich man in this parable may be seen as characteristic of the attitudes of those in hell. The rich man did not say to Lazarus, "Forgive me for my indifference and callousness to you"; he thought only of himself and his brothers. He was rueful and unhappy that he had come to the place of torment—but he had no words of repentance.

Another example of this can be seen in the experience of those who will suffer the seal judgments of the tribulation (Rev. 6:1–17). Even after it is obvious that these judgments are from God, the wicked will still not repent but will appeal to the mountains to fall on them to hide them from "the presence of Him who sits on the throne, and from the wrath of the Lamb" (6:16; see also Isa. 2:19). Just so, those in hell do not want to repent. There is no sign that those in hell—even then!—feel remorse or a desire to submit to the lordship and sovereignty of God. They will not—even then!—ask for His forgiveness. Since they have not had the gracious gift of repentance[9] given to them, they will continue to have the same rebellious attitude toward the Lord God and will persist in the same rejection of Christ they had in life.

Hell is an Eternal Place of Eternal Punishment

As noted, one of the most repeated objections to the biblical view of hell is that it is a place of eternal punishment. But in spite of attempts to redefine the terms, Scripture is quite clear that the punishment in hell is eternal, in the sense of unending, perpetual, and ceaseless. Jesus says that those who are *not* His faithful disciples "will go away into eternal punishment," but those

9 Repentance is a gift (Acts 11:18; 2 Tim. 2:25), as is faith (Eph. 2:8–9).

who are His true servants, whom He calls "the righteous," will go "into eternal life" (Matt. 25:46). Jesus uses (and Matthew records) the term "eternal" twice in this verse; it must mean the same thing in both usages. It has been noted previously that the "eternal life" of a believer is not simply unending life, but a *quality* of life, and an *ongoing experience* of that life. Thus, the punishment of the unbeliever is an *ongoing experience* of that punishment. This is the very meaning of the apostle John's words in Revelation 20:10 that the punishment in hell (the lake of fire) will be "day and night forever and ever."

Degrees of Punishment

Although all who enter hell will suffer eternal and terrible punishment, the Bible does indicate that there will be different degrees of punishment in hell. When Jesus denounced the cities of Chorazin and Bethsaida he told them that "if the miracles had occurred in Tyre and Sidon which occurred in you, they would have repented long ago in sackcloth and ashes" and so "it will be more tolerable for Tyre and Sidon in the day of judgment than for you" (Matt. 11:20–22). Likewise, in a similar rebuke He said to Capernaum, "if the miracles had occurred in Sodom which occurred in you, it would have remained to this day. Nevertheless, I say to you that it will be more tolerable for the land of Sodom in the day of judgment, than for you" (11:23–24). Tyre and Sidon were cities noted for corruption and cut-throat business practices, and Sodom was a horrible place of gross sin and debauchery (Gen. 19). But here Jesus says that the cities where He did miracles and preached would receive greater punishment than those notorious cities of corruption and vice. Those who hear the Word and reject it are more culpable and will be judged more severely than those who have never heard.

In another place Jesus asks the question,"Who then is the faithful and sensible steward . . . ?" (Luke 12:42). In answer, He pictures servants who are given responsibilities by a master but are negligent and unproductive. When that master returns, he will, of course, punish those faithless and neglectful servants. But Jesus adds this: "That slave who knew his master's will and did not get ready or act in accord with his will, will receive many lashes, but the one who did not know it, and committed deeds worthy of a flogging, will receive but few" (12:47–48). Here again is the principle that for those who know the will and Word of God and fail to obey it, there will be a harsher punishment than those who did not know.

The author of Hebrews also acknowledges this principle: "Anyone who has set aside the Law of Moses dies without mercy on the testimony of two or three witnesses" (Heb. 10:28). He goes on to ask, "How much severer punishment do you think he will deserve who has trampled under foot the Son of God, and has regarded as unclean the blood of the covenant by which he was sanctified, and has insulted the Spirit of grace?" (10:29). Predicting a "severer punishment" for anyone who rejects Christ acknowledges the principle of *proportional punishment*—that some offenses against God will be given a greater degree of punishment. This principle will be applied to the sinners in hell; all will justly suffer, but some will suffer more.

Hell is a Place of Retributive Justice

The punishment in hell is not for the purpose of rehabilitation of the sinner; the purpose is retributive justice, that is, it intends the punishment of sinners and does not intend deterrence or rehabilitation. God's justice demands the just punishment of sinners by the all-righteous God. God's justice is never arbitrary or vindictive. The Bible repeatedly affirms that God is just ("Shall not the Judge of all the earth deal justly?" Gen. 18:25), and will judge "in righteousness" (Acts 17:31). God's default inclination is to be longsuffering and forbearing, even in cases where the sin is greatly deserved (Exod. 34:6; Ps. 86:15). Indeed, even in the case of Sodom and Gomorrah, God reassured Abraham that He would forestall His just punishment of those wicked cities if even a few righteous persons could be found in them (Gen. 18:23–33). Still, even though "The LORD is slow to anger and abundant in lovingkindness," He "will by no means clear the guilty" (Num. 14:18).

It is appropriate here to point out that it is this punishment that Jesus Christ suffered on the cross as a sacrifice and substitute for sinners. Believers, like all sinners, deserve all the pain and suffering of hell, but because they have placed all their faith in Christ, they have the promise that He took all that pain and suffering on Himself on the cross. This is the truth the apostle Paul speaks of in Romans 5:6–10:

> For while we were still helpless, at the right time Christ died for the ungodly. For one will hardly die for a righteous person; though perhaps for the good man someone would even dare to die. But God demonstrates His own love toward us, in that while we were yet sinners, Christ died for us. Much more then, having now been justified by His blood, we shall be saved from the wrath of God through Him. For if while we were enemies we were reconciled to God through the death of His Son, much more, having been reconciled, we shall be saved by His life.

Paul also refers to this truth in Second Corinthians 5:21: "He made Him who knew no sin to be sin on our behalf, so that we might become the righteousness of God in Him." This is the doctrine of *penal substitutionary atonement* (taking, in the place of another, the penalty for their sin). Isaiah prophesized Christ's sacrificial death (hundreds of years before it happened!) in these terms: "But He was pierced through for our transgressions, / He was crushed for our iniquities; / The chastening for our well-being fell upon Him, / And by His scourging we are healed. / All of us like sheep have gone astray, / Each of us has turned to his own way; / But the LORD has caused the iniquity of us all / To fall on Him" (Isa. 53:5–6).

While no one can completely fathom the depth of Christ's suffering for the sins of everyone who would ever trust in Him, it is sobering to realize that it was when He bled, suffered, and died on the cross that all the pains of hell were placed on Him, so that believers would be delivered from those pains.

Hell is a Place of Eternal Separation from God

Even with these several descriptions of hell as a place of anguish, torment, and pain, the worst reality about hell is that it will be a place of separation from God. At the end of the Sermon on the Mount (Matt. 5–7), Jesus made this surprising, even shocking, statement, "Not everyone who says to Me, 'Lord, Lord,' will enter the kingdom of heaven" (7:21). What He meant by this warning is that there will be some, even many, who think they are right with Him, but who are, in fact, not right with Him. They have a mere profession of faith, but they do not possess a genuine faith. He even says, "I never knew you" (7:23). What He meant by that was, "I never had an intimate personal relationship with you; I never knew you as one of My sheep" (John 10:1–14). For all those He does not know—those who make a false profession of faith, as well as all those who never claimed to know Him—Jesus made this chilling command: "Depart from Me" (Matt. 7:23; Ps. 6:8). Jesus uses this same expression in Matthew 25:41: "Depart from Me, accursed ones," and He specifies there that this departure is "into the eternal fire which has been prepared for the devil and his angels." This is a departure "into eternal punishment" (Matt. 25:46); it is a departure to "eternal destruction, away from the presence of the Lord and from the glory of His power" (2 Thess. 1:9).

Of course, in one sense, even in hell men and women will not be totally away from God's presence—since He is and always will be omnipresent, everywhere present. But in hell there will be no benevolent presence, no joyous fellowship, no personal communion with God.

SUMMARY ON HELL

These affirmations about hell drawn from Scripture are not intended to paint a definitive picture of hell or help us create a scale model of hell, much less draw a blueprint of its compartments or a roadmap of its streets. They are revealed in the Bible solely to make it clear to one and all that hell is real—and is really horrific. These descriptions should encourage the reader to turn in repentance from sin, and to place their faith in Jesus Christ, the only One who can save us from the fires of hell.

For believers, the reality of hell should cause us to be supremely grateful to God for graciously drawing us to Himself and for the sin-covering atonement and forgiveness of the cross of Christ; it should cause us to be sober, sorrowful, and distressed for unbelievers who are on the wide path to destruction (Matt. 7:13); it should cause us to be more compassionate, and therefore more bold, to preach the gospel of Christ to the lost (see Appendix A). The believer can never afford to be indifferent about hell, much less flippant about hell, and very much less triumphant about hell.

Study Questions:

1. What are the views of those who deny the biblical doctrine of hell?
2. How do the terms *gehenna* and lake of fire contribute to the biblical picture of hell?
3. What are the various aspects to the biblical picture of hell, as described in this chapter?
4. Why do some think there are degrees of punishment in hell?
5. What kind of "justice" is meted out in hell, or what is the nature of the punishment?

8

Death and the Believer

Even though the believer does not have the fear and dread of death that unbelievers do, death is still a sad reality which they will face for themselves and their loved ones in Christ. There will come that time when each believer must "walk through the valley of the shadow of death" (Ps. 23:4), and until then believers must deal with the loss of loved ones "who have fallen asleep in Jesus" (1 Thess. 4:14).

So, even for believers, death is still a cause for grief. Even for believers, death is sad and odious. Acts 8:2 records that there was lamentation over Stephen's death. Mary, the sister of Lazarus, wept for her deceased brother (John 11:33). To be sure, believers do not "grieve as do the rest who have no hope" (1 Thess. 4:13), but even in those very hopeful words from the apostle Paul there is the recognition, that indeed, they still grieve. There is sadness for the time of separation from loved ones. It is not wrong for believers to mourn the death of a loved one, or to be apprehensive at the approach of death. The Psalms speak honestly about death. In Psalm 18 David cried out to God, "The cords of death encompassed me, / And the torrents of ungodliness terrified me. / The cords of Sheol surrounded me; / The snares of death confronted me" (Ps. 18:4–5). Clearly, David faced the possibility of death with concern and anxiety; nevertheless, the entire psalm is a testimony to hope and confidence in God.

So it is not inappropriate for a believer to feel anxious about death (no one wants to die!) while at the same time holding on to his or her complete confidence in God's promises of eternal life and the hope of going to heaven. In Psalm 55 David even goes so far as to speak of "the terrors of death," which he says "have fallen upon me" (55:4); but in the next psalm, he affirms his trust and confidence in God: "When I am afraid, / I will put my trust in You. / In God, whose word I praise, / In God I have put my trust; / I shall not be afraid" (56:3–4). Believers are not immune to the misfortunes and calamities that are the existential experiences of all human beings living in a Genesis 3 (fallen and corrupt) world; and that includes death. And so believers are encouraged to "weep with those who weep" (Rom. 12:15); at the grave of Lazarus, "Jesus wept" (John 11:35). In short, the believer is not required to live in denial; the prospect of death is not delightful and the loss of a loved one to death (even a believer) is a cause for sorrow. In Philippians 2:27, Paul said that the near-death of Epaphroditus, who had been "sick to the point of death," would have brought "sorrow upon sorrow" to the apostle.

But the believer has an assured hope and therefore great confidence in the face of death.

The Metaphors of Death for a Believer

In spite of the inevitability of physical death, death for the believer is not the utter terror and unmitigated tragedy that it is for the unbeliever. The Bible describes death for the believer with several metaphors which, when fully understood, provide a perspective on death that mitigates, or even eliminates, "the sting of death" (1 Cor. 15:56).

A Falling Asleep

It was noted in Chapter 4, in the discussion of "soul sleep," that in several texts Scripture uses the metaphor of "sleeping" to describe the state or experience of believers after death. It was noted there that these texts cannot be used to argue for the notion of "soul sleep," as many false religions and cults teach. However, the misuse of the metaphor should not detract from its proper use and meaning in the Bible.

The are several texts in the Old Testament where "sleep" is used metaphorically of death. In Psalm 13:3 David, in a time of trouble, laments, "Consider and answer me, O Lord my God; / Enlighten my eyes, or I will sleep the sleep of death." In Jeremiah 51:57 the prophet speaks the word of judgment of "The Lord of hosts" that the governors, prefects, and mighty men of Babylon will "sleep a perpetual sleep and not wake up"—meaning, of course, they will all be dead. These instances (and similar texts such as Job 7:21 and 14:10–12) emphasize that death is a termination of temporal existence with no earthly prospect of reversal.

Another Old Testament text uses the metaphor of "sleep" for death in a way that does not view death as a terminal or hopeless state. In Daniel 12:1, the prophet writes of a far future time of distress for his people, the Jews, followed by the restoration of the nation: "And there will be a time of distress such as never occurred since there was a nation until that time; and at that time your people, everyone who is found written in the book, will be rescued."[1] This restoration will then be followed by a time of resurrection and judgment. "Many of those who sleep in the dust of the ground will awake, these to everlasting life, but the others to disgrace and everlasting contempt" (Dan. 12:2). There will be more on the matter of these resurrections in the following chapters, but here the point to be noted is that, for Daniel at least, the metaphor of "sleep" was not absolutely terminal; it was not final, but was an experience from which many "will awake." It should be noted that Daniel says this "sleep" is "in the dust of the ground," which alludes to the burial of the body.

In sum, it may be said that when these texts use the metaphor of "sleep" for death as a terminal for earthly, temporal existence and it is best to understand this as applying to physical bodies. Daniel's use of the metaphor indicates that this is a "sleep" from which many will awake.

This metaphor of "sleep" for death is used in the New Testament of Stephen (Acts 7:60), of believers who were disciplined (1 Cor. 11:30), and of believers who have died but will not miss the Rapture (15:6, 18, 20; 1 Thess. 4:13–14). But again this "sleep" is meant to refer to the physical body, in hope of an awakening when the resurrection body (see the discussion on the believers' resurrection body in Chapter 9) of believers is reunited with their souls/spirits. In short, between the physical death and the resurrection to come, the bodies of believers are in a temporary condition—like sleep. This is a hopeful metaphor, that, while it acknowledges the reality of the physical death of believers, it anticipates an awakening with a resurrection body.

A Departure

Another metaphor found in Scripture speaks of death as a departure. At the transfiguration, Moses and Elijah appeared with Jesus and they "were speaking of His departure which He was about to accomplish at Jerusalem" (Luke 9:31); this, of course, referred to His passion—His death and resurrection. Jesus would die, but be raised, and in the Ascension, He would depart to His Father in heaven.

This metaphor is used by the apostle Paul in Philippians 1. In the apostle's great affirmation of faith in Christ he declared, "For to me, to live is Christ and to die is gain" (Phil. 1:21). Here he unequivocally declares his

---

1 This time of distress is the tribulation and the time of restoration is the millennial kingdom; for more details of this chronology see Appendix B: A Dispensational, Premillennial Overview of End-Time Events.

confidence in life after death; his death would be neither a loss, nor a terminal ending, but a gain; it would be a positive benefit, a profitable result, even a reward. But, as he continues to ponder his immediate prospects, he writes, "But I am hard-pressed from both directions, having the desire to depart and be with Christ, for that is very much better; yet to remain on in the flesh is more necessary for your sake" (Phil. 1:23–24). Paul considered that his death would simply be a "departure" with the confident expectation of something "very much better" than continued temporal existence on earth.

Paul again uses the metaphor of death as a departure in his second letter to his "son in the faith," Timothy. This epistle is likely the last letter written by the apostle and it is clear he expected to be martyred soon, since he referred to his impending death: "For I am already being poured out as a drink offering, and the time of my departure has come" (2 Tim. 4:6). Here he uses two metaphors to speak of his death. First, he regards his death as a sacrifice of his life like a drink offering which is poured out (Phil. 2:17; Exod. 29:40; Num. 15:4–6, 10) for Christ. Second, he views his death as a departure; the Greek term (found only here in the New Testament) is *analyesōs*, and has the connotation of a "release," as if Paul is being unbound and thus free to advance.

In sum, the metaphor of death as a departure evokes a passage from one state to another and in these cases that is a departure from this life on earth to the next life in heaven. When one makes a "departure" he or she has a destination in mind. For a believer the departure from this earthly existence has a heavenly destination in mind.

The Vacating of a Deteriorated Dwelling and Occupying a Lasting One

Another metaphor of movement or passage sees death as the vacating of a deteriorating dwelling and the occupying of another, more lasting dwelling. The apostle Paul uses this metaphor of in Second Corinthians 5.

> For we know that if the earthly tent which is our house is torn down, we have a building from God, a house not made with hands, eternal in the heavens. For indeed in this house we groan, longing to be clothed with our dwelling from heaven, inasmuch as we, having put it on, will not be found naked. For indeed while we are in this tent, we groan, being burdened, because we do not want to be unclothed but to be clothed, so that what is mortal will be swallowed up by life. (2 Cor. 5:1–4)

In these four verses Paul actually employs two related metaphors. In the first verse he refers to his earthly, physical body as "the earthly tent" and, he says, this is "our house." A tent is not only a temporary dwelling, by design but also, like all earthly dwellings, it is subject to deterioration. Paul realistically knows this "earthly tent which is our house" may (indeed, will!) be "torn down"—that is, these bodies, wear out over time, or are destroyed by other forces. Paul was often threatened with death by his opponents (Acts 14:19; 22:22; 23:12–21; 2 Cor. 1:9), and he was often in circumstances that endangered his life (Acts 27:14–44; 2 Cor. 1:10; 11:23–27). He lived constantly with the possibility of death, so his words about the "groaning" that comes from the wear-and-tear and stress on the physical body are not hyperbole in his case. In the context preceding the verses quoted above, Paul speaks of his "outer man" (that is, his body) as "decaying"—in the process of breaking down—as if it were already a dead body.

But as Paul continues in that same verse (5:1), he affirms that "we have a building from God, a house not made with hands, eternal in the heavens." That dwelling will not be a temporary tent but a lasting, eternal dwelling. Here, it seems, is where Paul mixes his metaphors. He was speaking of the earthly physical body, but now it seems he is declaring that God has a heavenly abode or dwelling in mind. It is best, however, to see the references to a "house" in both instances as a body—one the earthly, physical body and the other a heavenly body ("eternal in the heavens"). Each body is then also referred to by Paul as a dwelling—one is a tent, presumably made by human hands and the other is a "building from God," "not made with [human] hands."

So taking the several verses of Second Corinthians 5:1–4 together, Paul is saying the first body-house is earthly, is being torn down (decaying), because it is made of inferior materials (as tent is made of fabric), by inferior workmen; it is a burden ("being burdened," 5:4); it is mortal ("so that what is mortal," 5:4)—it will die. On the other hand, there is the second body-house which is fitted for heaven, and lasting ("eternal in the heavens," 5:1); it is a "building from God" (as such it would presumably be made of superior materials and set on lasting foundations); it is just the suitable "clothing" (5:2, 4) for heavenly life; and it puts an end to our "groaning."

In sum, Paul's metaphor may be complicated, but his meaning is clear: believers may be dealing with earthly bodies that are decaying and are subject to death, but they have the promise of a heavenly body (see Chapter 9 on the resurrection body) and a heavenly dwelling (John 14:2–3). In that heavenly body believers will no longer deal with the groaning that is the experience of everyone in this temporal sphere.

The apostle Peter also employs this metaphor briefly in his second letter. In the first chapter, as he is admonishing and reminding his readers of their resources and obligations as believers, he explains, "I consider it right, as long as I am in this earthly dwelling, to stir you up by way of reminder, knowing that the laying aside of my earthly dwelling is imminent, as also our Lord Jesus Christ has made clear to me" (2 Pet. 1:13–14). For Peter, as for Paul, the "earthly dwelling" is his physical body, which he expects to "lay aside" soon. In the next verse, Peter uses the "death as a departure" metaphor, "And I will also be diligent that at any time after my departure you will be able to call these things to mind" (1:15). Peter is, in effect, giving his final admonitions to his readers, and his impending departure (from the earthly dwelling to a heavenly one) makes these admonitions more poignant.

A Going to A Heavenly Home

One of the most precious metaphors used for the death of a believer, one that is related to the two above, is the metaphor of death as a homegoing. Probably no metaphor for death is more familiar or more often referenced than this.

The wording is based on Second Corinthians 5:6–8: "Therefore, being always of good courage, and knowing that while we are at home in the body we are absent from the Lord—for we walk by faith, not by sight—we are of good courage, I say, and prefer rather to be absent from the body and to be at home with the Lord." Paul asserts that as long as believers are in this life—"in the body"—they are "absent from the Lord." This does not mean believers are without the fellowship and lordship of Jesus in this life. He promised "lo, I am with you always" (Matt. 28:20); He sent His Spirit to guide and comfort believers (John 14:16–17, 26; 15:26); and He has given them His Word. But even though believers do not see Him now (1 Pet. 1:8) they live with the promise that they will see Him (1 John 3:2) at His coming. What Paul means here is that believers who die will immediately go to be with Jesus, to live with Him in the "dwelling places" He is preparing for His bride (John 14:2). This metaphor of death as a homegoing is very much along the lines of the last verse of the beloved Psalm 23: "Surely goodness and lovingkindness will follow me all the days of my life, / And I will dwell in the house of the LORD forever" (Ps. 23:6).

THE BELIEVER'S PERSPECTIVE ON DEATH

Death cannot separate believers from God's Love

One of the best loved chapters in the New Testament is Romans 8. It is not, perhaps, among the best known generally, but many Christians who are more than superficially familiar with the books of the New Testament, and particularly with the epistles of the apostle Paul, will list Romans 8 as a favorite. The reasons for this are many. To begin with this chapter opens with, "Therefore there is now no condemnation for those who are in Christ Jesus. For the law of the Spirit of life in Christ Jesus has set you free from the law of sin and death" (8:1–2). This is a promise of freedom from the condemnation of the law which Paul has argued cannot set us "free from the body of this death" (7:24). The law can only condemn, and that condemnation brings about our death. But Paul exclaims, there is no condemnation in Christ Jesus! That is, no condemnation for those who are justified.

Paul continues in that chapter to explain that those who are delivered from condemnation are indwelt by the Spirit and have the promise of glory (8:8–17). This prospect of glory, Paul says, should encourage believers to persevere even in the face of suffering and hardship in this life. "For I consider that the sufferings of this present time are not worthy to be compared with the glory that is to be revealed to us" (8:18; see also 8:19–25). Paul then speaks of the ministry of the Spirit (8:26–27) as well as giving one of the most precious promises to persevering believers in verse 28: "And we know that God causes all things to work together for good to those who love God, to those who are called according to His purpose." This promise is followed by the equally precious truths that the believer was foreknown and predestined for salvation, and that he or she will ultimately be glorified (8:29–30).

All of this is made possible because "God is for us," and He "did not spare His own Son, but delivered Him over for us all" (8:31–32). This, as Paul writes, reassures us as believers that God will withhold no blessing from us but will "freely give us all things" (8:32). Since God sovereignly elected us and freely justified us (3:21–26), and since Christ died for us and now intercedes for us (8:33–34), the believer can be sure that nothing will separate us from the love of Christ (8:35) and "in all these things we overwhelmingly conquer through Him who loved us" (8:37).

But do all those promises, reassurances, and blessings end with the believer's death? The great climax of Romans 8 affirms the truth that even death does not separate the believer from God's love in Christ. "For I am convinced that *neither death*, nor life, nor angels, nor principalities, nor things present, nor things to come, nor powers, nor height, nor depth, nor any other created thing will be able to separate us from the love of God that is in Christ Jesus our Lord" (8:38–39).

Death is a Victory over a Conquered Enemy

The great text on the resurrection in First Corinthians 15 will be considered in detail in Chapter 10. For now it is important to state that, according to verses 54 to 57, death is a conquered enemy and believers have the promise of victory over death. In these verses the apostle Paul assures believers who live in hope of the resurrection that "Death is swallowed up in victory," that death has lost its "sting," and so, "thanks to be God," believers have "the victory through our Lord Jesus Christ." For believers, death is not so much a loss as it is a victory; not an ending but a beginning; not a woeful prospect of utter loss or a dreadful prospect of future pain and judgment, but a transition to a place of bliss (see Chapter 11), a reunion with those who have died in Christ.

This is why the apostle Paul can say of death, "For to me, to live is Christ and to die is gain" (Phil. 1:21). Physical death means "to be absent from the body" but it also means "to be at home with the Lord" (2 Cor. 5:8). The death of a believer brings about the greatest blessing imaginable, namely, entrance into the presence of Christ which will be "very much better" (Phil. 1:23) than anything this passing temporal world can offer. Death is not something to be feared (as it is for those "who have no hope," 1 Thess. 4:13), but it is the realization of the promise in Psalm 23:6 that the believer will "dwell in the house of the LORD forever."

Study Questions:

1. How is the grief of believers in the face of death different than the grief of unbelievers?

2. Why does a believer have confidence and hope even in the face of death?

3. What are the metaphors in Scripture of the believer's experience of death?

4. What is the believer's perspective on death (as outlined in this chapter)?

9

The Believer's Hope of Resurrection

THE BELIEVER'S ULTIMATE hope of eternal fellowship with God and Christ is not hope for a purely spiritual experience. The Christian does not look forward to an eternal disembodied existence but to a bodily resurrection on the pattern of Christ's own bodily resurrection.

The believer's hope will be considered in this and the next chapter. However, before turning to the reality of the believer's hope of the rapture (see Chapter 10, especially the sections on First Thessalonians 4:13–18 and First Corinthians 15), it will be most helpful to consider the more general topic of resurrection under three headings: The Resuscitations in the Bible, The Resurrection of Jesus Christ as the Pattern for The Believer's Resurrection, and The Whole Eschatological Program of the Resurrections.

The Resuscitations in the Bible

The idea of "resurrection" must be distinguished from that of "resuscitation." Instances of resuscitation occurred in the Old Testament and in the New Testament.

Old Testament Instances

There are several accounts, in both testaments, of people who had died but were raised up to life once more. In the era of the prophets Elijah and Elisha, three people who had died were brought back to life. During the drought which came on Israel in the reign of the wicked king Ahab (1 Kings 17), Elijah was commanded to "go to Zarephath, which belongs to Sidon, and stay there" because the Lord had "commanded a widow there to provide for" Elijah (17:9). The prophet and the widow and her son were sustained from a "bowl of flour" and a small "jar of oil" that miraculously did not run out for many days (17:14–16). However, "it came about after these things that the son of the woman, the mistress of the house, became sick; and his sickness was so severe that there was no breath left in him" (1 Kings 17:17). The distraught woman turned to the prophet, who took the boy to his own room and laid him on his own bed (17:19). Elijah prayed to the Lord, and "Then he stretched himself upon the child three times, and called to the Lord and said, 'O Lord my God, I pray You, let this child's life return to him'" (17:21). The Lord's answer was swift and positive: "The Lord heard the voice of Elijah, and the life of the child returned to him and he revived" (17:22).

There is little question that the lad had actually died, since Elijah prayed for the boy's life (Hebrew, *nephesh*) to return to him. This term *nephesh* was used in Gen. 2:7 to describe how Adam "became a living being" after "the Lord God formed man of dust from the ground, and breathed into his nostrils the breath of life." When the life of the son of the widow "returned (Hebrew, *shub*) to him" he came back to life. But this was a return to a state of life that he had before; he regained his physical life. This was not a resurrection to a new condition, a new life, or a new state of existence, such as Paul describes in First Corinthians 15 (see more on this in Chapter 10).

A similar occurrence happened in the ministry of Elisha as recorded in Second Kings 4. In the course of his travels, Elisha was befriended and provided for by a well-to-do woman and her husband of the village of Shunem (4:8). This woman persuaded her husband to set up a room with furniture in their home as a place for the prophet to stay and rest when he was in Shunem (4:9). This couple had no son, and so, as a blessing for them for the kindness they had shown him, the prophet promised that they would have a son within a year; and so they did (4:16–17). However, one day when the son had grown and was in the field helping with the harvest, he inexplicably cried out to his father, "My head, my head" (4:19). He was carried to his mother, but sadly, "he sat on her lap until noon, and then died" (4:20). The woman "laid [her son] on the bed of the man of God" and quickly rode a donkey by herself to go to Elisha (4:21–25). When she finally arrived to speak to Elisha he could see she was distraught, and when he learned of her son's condition he sent his servant, Gehazi, ahead with his staff in order to lay it on the boy's face, but this only confirmed that "there was no sound or response" (4:31).

Indeed, when he arrived, "Elisha came into the house, behold the lad was dead and laid on his bed" (4:32). Again, as with the son of the widow of Zarephath, there was no question that this child was dead. After Elisha prayed he laid down on the boy and "he put his mouth on his mouth and his eyes on his eyes and his hands on his hands, and he stretched himself on him" and with this the flesh of the child became warm (4:33–34). Elisha continued this a second time, and then "the lad sneezed seven times and the lad opened his eyes" (2 Kings 4:35), and was reunited with his mother (4:36–37). Once again, this was a resuscitation to life as the mother and son had known it. There is every reason to assume that this son was restored to a normal physical existence in his own temporal body—not a resurrection in a new body.

An even stranger revival of physical life is recorded in Second Kings 13. After Elisha had died and was buried (13:20), a group of Moabites were at the same time burying one of their own. They saw a band of marauders coming, so they hastily cast the dead man's body into the open grave of Elisha. It must have been quite a shock for them to witness that "when the [body of the dead] man touched the bones of Elisha he revived and stood up on his feet" (13:21).

New Testament Instances in the Life of Jesus

There are three recorded instances of resuscitation in Jesus' ministry: Jairus' daughter (Matt. 9:18–19, 23–25; Mark 5:21–24, 35–43; Luke 8:40–42, 49–56), the young man at Nain (Luke 7:14), and that of Lazarus (John 11:38–44). In the first instance, an official of the synagogue (Matt. 9:18; Luke 8:41, literally a "ruler") named Jairus (Mark 5:22) came to Jesus because his daughter was "at the point of death" (Mark 5:23; Luke 8:42). In fact, as Matthew records the account, the man said, "My daughter has just died"; Jairus pleaded for Jesus to come to his house because he had faith that if Jesus would lay His hand on her "she will live" (Matt. 9:18).

Jesus responded immediately but was delayed by a woman who had suffered from "a hemorrhage for twelve years" (9:20), who wanted to be healed and believed that merely touching His clothes would heal her (9:21). This the woman managed to do—and she was healed! But Jesus took notice of her act of faith (Luke 8:45–47) and took a brief moment to acknowledge her and commend her faith (Matt. 9:22; Mark 5:34; Luke 8:48).

However, even this brief delay was consequential for, as Luke records, "While he was still speaking" to the woman the news arrived that Jairus' daughter had died (Mark 5:35; Luke 8:49). Jesus, nevertheless, encouraged the synagogue official to "only believe" and proceeded to the house where the little girl was lying. When He arrived, and He saw the commotion, the noisy mourners, the lamentation, and the weeping, He assured them that the child had not died, but was only asleep (Matt. 9:24; Mark 5:39; Luke 8:52). Jesus was not denying the fact that the child had died. That was undeniable and was the reason why those mourners "began laughing at Him, knowing that she had died" (Luke 8:53; see also Matt. 9:24; Mark 5:40).

Jesus could speak as He did because He knew He was about to restore her to life. Having sent the mourners out, with only the child's parents and His disciples, Jesus tenderly took her hand (Matt. 9:25; Mark 5:40–41; Luke 8:51, 54) and said, "'Talitha kum!' (which translated means 'Little girl, I say to you, get up!' And immediately the girl got up" (Mark 5:41; Matt. 9:25). Luke adds this important note: "her spirit returned" (Luke 8:55), which further indicates that the girl was indeed dead but was resuscitated to the life she had with her parents. Also, Luke records that Jesus "ordered that something be given her to eat" (8:55). In this setting Jesus' order also indicated that the little girl had been restored to a normal physical life—she needed food to regain her strength.

The account of the raising of the son of a widow from the town of Nain is recorded only in Luke's gospel (Luke 7:11–17). In this instance, Jesus happened upon a funeral procession for a young man, "the only son of his mother" (7:12). Luke records that when Jesus saw this widow, He felt compassion for her "and said to her, 'Do not weep'" (7:13). He stopped the procession by touching the coffin (7:14), which was unusual because, according to some rabbinic interpretations of the Law, it would have made Jesus ritually unclean. Jesus then spoke to the dead man and said, "'Young man, I say to you, arise!' And the dead man sat up and began to speak"; and then He "gave him back to his mother" (7:14–15). Nothing else is known about this man or his mother; presumably, as with the other cases noted previously, he returned to the normal, physical existence he had known before he had died.

New Testament Instances in the Ministry of the Apostles

There are two instances of someone being raised in the book of Acts: the resurrection of Tabitha (also called Dorcas) in Acts 9:36–42 and the resurrection of a young man named Eutychus in Acts 20:7–12. Again, these are instances of *resuscitation*, not a *resurrection* to new life, which is the hope of the believer.

The Resurrection of Jesus Christ as the Pattern for The Believer's Resurrection

Before considering God's resurrection plans for all of mankind, it is necessary to briefly consider Christ's resurrection. The resurrection of Christ is called "the first fruits" (1 Cor. 15:23), because His resurrection is the pattern for the other resurrections to come, especially the resurrections of believers.

A number of details from the resurrection accounts in the Gospels and Acts are pertinent to an understanding of the believer's hope of resurrection.

The most obvious detail to note is that the tomb was empty (Luke 24:12) and the body of Jesus was not there: "But on the first day of the week, at early dawn, they [the women, Mark 16:1] came to the tomb bringing the spices which they had prepared. And they found the stone rolled away from the tomb, but when they entered, they did not find the body of the Lord Jesus" (Luke 24:1–3). The angel explained this by saying that "He is not here, for He has risen, just as He said. Come, see the place where He was lying" (Matt. 28:6; see also Mark 16:56; Luke 24:5–6). This detail reveals that His resurrection was bodily.

Resurrection Accounts in the Gospels

In Matthew's account, after this encounter with the angel (Matt. 28:2, 5), or angels (Luke 24:2; John 20:12), Jesus "met . . . and greeted" (Matt. 28:9) the women (Mark 16:9), and it seems that the women recognized Him. However, as John records the conversation with Mary Magdalene at first, while she saw a man (John 20:14) and she supposed it was a gardener (20:15) she "did not know that it was Jesus" (20:14). But as the conversation continued, in fact as Jesus spoke Mary's name (20:16) she did recognize Him, and "She turned and said to Him in Hebrew, 'Rabboni!' (which means, Teacher)" (20:16). These details indicate that His resurrection body appeared in a normal human male form such that He could be mistaken for an ordinary gardener, and then recognized as the man Mary knew before His crucifixion and burial.

Luke records that later that day two others (one of whom was named Cleopas, Luke 24:18) had an encounter with Jesus (24:13–15). As they were walking together they were discussing "these things which had taken place," that is "the things" about the life and works of Jesus, as well as His crucifixion and His resurrection (24:14, 19–24). Luke records that while "their eyes were prevented from recognizing Him" (24:16), Jesus met these two on the road to Emmaus and continued this conversation about "The things about Jesus the Nazarene" (24:19). Jesus corrected their misunderstanding and "Then beginning with Moses and with all the prophets, He explained to them the things concerning Himself in all the Scriptures" (24:27). Still unaware of the identity of their master-teacher, having arrived at their destination, the two persuaded Him to join them for lodging and a dinner (24:28–29). It was at this dinner, at the moment when He broke the bread and offered a blessing (24:30), that "their eyes were opened and they recognized Him." However, no doubt much to their surprise, that very moment "He vanished from their sight" (24:31). The details of this encounter reaffirm that His resurrection body appeared in a normal human male form such that He could be taken for a fellow traveler and dinner guest. However, the detail that "He vanished from their sight" indicates that this body was not limited in the ways an earthly body is limited.

Summary

What do these narratives teach about Christ's resurrection that also tell us about the resurrections of believers to come?

Jesus' resurrection was not a mere resuscitation, like those in the ministries of Elijah and Elisha in the Old Testament, or in the ministries of Jesus, Peter, and Paul in the New. There is no indication to imagine that the young men raised by Elijah and Elisha, or the daughter of Jairus, or the son of the widow of Nain, or Lazarus, or Dorcus, or Eutychus, lived anything but a normal lifespan after their astounding revivifications—that they did not eventually succumb to a normal death. Scripture records nothing unusual about them after these remarkable resuscitations.

The resurrection of Jesus is different in a number of ways. After His resurrection, as the details noted above have shown, Jesus could and did appear as a normal human male. He could converse with others, He could touch and be touched by others, He could even eat fish. Yet, He could vanish and appear in that body and He could be transported in that body into the presence of His Father.

Paul indicates that Jesus' resurrection body is different than the body of His temporal, physical existence. This comes out in his encouragement of the Philippians in these words: "For our citizenship is in heaven, from which also we eagerly wait for a Savior, the Lord Jesus Christ; who will transform the body of our humble state into conformity with the body of His glory, by the exertion of the power that He has even to subject all things to Himself" (Phil. 3:20–21). Paul is telling the believers in Philippi that Jesus' resurrection body is a body of glory, a body fit for glory. Paul says the believer is promised just such a body; a body that will be transformed (Greek: *metaschēmatisei*, "changed in fashion or appearance") to conform (Greek: *symmorphon*, "sharing the same inner essence-identity") to His body. The believer's resurrection body will be precisely the body needed to live where our citizenship is—heaven.

The Whole Eschatological Program of the Resurrections

The Bible reveals that God's resurrection plans for all of mankind will take place at various times for various groups of people. It is necessary to study the relevant texts carefully to discern the timing and subjects of the various resurrections of Scripture.

Passages such as Daniel 12:2, John 5:28–29, and Romans 2:5–8 explicitly state that there will be a resurrection of the righteous and of the wicked. But does this mean that both groups will be resurrected at the same time? Some think it does, others that it does not. The position of this book is that the resurrection program occurs in stages. Just as there are phases to other aspects of God's program such as covenants, the Kingdom, salvation, and the day of the Lord, the judgments of Scripture occur in phases as well.

Two Key Passages about the Resurrections

Two key passages explicitly reveal an order in the resurrection program. First, Paul mentions three phases in First Corinthians 15:22–24.

> For as in Adam all die, so also in Christ all will be made alive. But each in his own order: Christ the first fruits, after that those who are Christ's at His coming, then comes the end, when He hands over the kingdom to the God and Father, when He has abolished all rule and all authority and power.

Second, the apostle John tells of two resurrections separated by a thousand years. In Revelation 20:4–5, he writes concerning certain martyrs, "They came to life and reigned with Christ for a thousand years. The rest of the dead did not come to life until the thousand years were completed." Note that there is one group that comes to life (i.e., is resurrected) and reigns with Christ for a thousand years, and then there is another group called "the rest of the dead," who are not resurrected until the thousand years runs its course. This shows two resurrections separated by a thousand years. So, then, two Bible passages explicitly teach stages in the resurrection program. When viewed together, they describe four phases of resurrection activity.

As noted, First Corinthians 15:20–24 reveals that Jesus Christ's resurrection is called the "first fruits." This resurrection (which happened historically around AD 30) was the first phase of the resurrection program; His resurrection was the "first fruits" of what is to come. His bodily resurrection serves as the template and guarantee for the resurrection of all who believe in Him.

The second phase of the resurrection—"those who are Christ's at His coming"—involves those who are raised in connection with the second coming of Jesus. This includes resurrected church saints, both dead and alive, at the rapture as described in First Thessalonians 4:14–17. At the rapture, the dead in Christ will rise first, and then living saints will be "caught up" to meet Jesus in the air. (There is more on this in Chapter 10.)

While not occurring at the time of the rapture, this third phase includes resurrected Old Testament saints (Dan. 12:2) and martyred saints during the tribulation period (Rev. 20:4). They experience resurrection when Jesus returns to earth. Revelation 6:9–11 tells of martyrs who gave their lives because of their testimony for Jesus. These souls in heaven call out for the avenging of their blood on earth but are told to wait a little while. Revelation 20:4 is the fulfillment of their expectation: "They came to life and reigned with Christ for a thousand years."

The fourth phase of the resurrection is what Paul calls "the end." This occurs after the millennial reign of Jesus. According to Revelation 20:5, this involves "the rest of the dead," who in this context are unbelievers, those destined for the great white throne judgment (20:11–15). So unbelievers are present at the resurrection after the thousand year reign of Christ. But do any believers experience resurrection at this fourth stage of the resurrection program? This is more difficult to answer, but they might, for the following reason. Non-glorified saints will enter the millennial kingdom as a result of being saved during the seven-year tribulation period. These are non-glorified saints who bore children with non-glorified bodies during the millennial kingdom (Isa. 65:20, 23). However, since First Corinthians 15:50 states that non-glorified bodies cannot enter God's eternal kingdom, these saints must receive glorified bodies at some point. It is likely that these non-glorified saints will receive resurrection bodies immediately at death or at the end of the millennium.

Five Conclusions about the Resurrections

Bringing all this together, five conclusions can be offered concerning the order of resurrections:

1. The Bible speaks of the resurrection of the redeemed as "the first resurrection" (Rev. 20:5), the "resurrection of life" (John 5:29), "eternal life" (Rom. 2:7), or "everlasting life" (Dan. 12:2).
2. This "first resurrection" of the redeemed occurs in three phases:

   a. Christ the first fruits (1 Cor. 15:23);
   b. church saints (15:23, 50–58; 1 Thess. 4:13–18);
   c. Old Testament saints (Ezek. 37:12–14; Dan. 12:2) along with tribulation saints (Rev. 20:4).
3. The Bible does not use the term "second resurrection" but refers to the resurrection of the unredeemed (unbelievers) as "a resurrection of judgment" (John 5:29) or "the second death" (Rev. 20:6, 14; 21:8).
4. The Bible gives no warrant to conclude that only one general resurrection of the righteous will occur at the end.
5. Thus, there are four recognized times of resurrection in Scripture:
   a. Christ's resurrection (1 Cor. 15:23);
   b. church saints' resurrection (15:23, 50–58; 1 Thess. 4:13–18);
   c. the resurrection of Old Testament saints (Ezek. 37:12–14; Dan. 12:2) and tribulation saints (Rev. 20:4); and
   d. the resurrection of the unredeemed of all time (Rev. 20:5).

Study Questions:

1. What is resuscitation? What are some examples of resuscitation in the Bible?

2. What do the biblical accounts of the Resurrection of Jesus teach about the very idea of resurrection?

3. What are the three phases of the whole end-times resurrection program as Paul describes in First Corinthians 15:22–24?

4. Summarize the conclusions noted concerning the order of resurrections in the Bible.

10

The Believer's Hope of the Rapture

THE WORD "HOPE" IN English does not quite capture the New Testament concept. The Greek word for hope, *elpizō*, does not mean merely a wish, but a "confident expectation" or "solid assurance."[1] The apostle Paul captures the idea very well in the simple affirmation "hope does not disappoint" (Rom. 5:5).

The "Blessed Hope" of the Church

Several passages in the New Testament speak about the "Blessed Hope" of the rapture of the church. The expression "blessed hope" is found in Titus 2:11–14, in which the apostle Paul affirms the three stages of the believer's salvation.

> For the grace of God has appeared, bringing salvation to all men, instructing us to deny ungodliness and worldly desires and to live sensibly, righteously and godly in the present age, looking for the blessed hope and the appearing of the glory of our great God and Savior, Christ Jesus, who gave Himself for us to redeem us from every lawless deed, and to purify for Himself a people for His own possession, zealous for good deeds.

The believer's salvation is "by grace" (Titus 2:11; Eph. 2:8–9), through the work of Christ Jesus, who "gave Himself" as a sacrifice on the cross (1 Pet. 2:24; Isa. 53:4; 1 Cor. 15:3) and whose death accomplished redemption (Titus 2:14; Rom. 3:24; Gal. 3:13). The believers (also called redeemed or saved) are to "deny ungodliness and worldly desires and to live sensibly, righteously and godly" (Titus 2:12) and live in the "blessed hope" of "the appearing of the glory of our great God and Savior, Christ Jesus" (2:13). This appearing of Christ will come first for the church at the rapture.

1 William D. Mounce, ed., Mounce's Complete Expository Dictionary of Old and New Testament Words (Grand Rapids, MI: Zondervan, 2006) s.v. "Hope," 340.

This coming for the church was first promised by Jesus Himself, in His so-called "Farewell Discourse" (John 14–16). In John 14:1 Jesus—knowing He was soon to leave them—reassured His disciples, "'Do not let your heart be troubled; believe in God, believe also in Me." He told them that He was going to His Father's house (heaven) to prepare a place for them (John 14:2–3). But He added this promise, "if I go and prepare a place for you, I will come again and receive you to Myself, that where I am, there you may be also" (14:3). This promise to "come again" is very different than the promise He made, and description He gave, of the Second Coming in Matthew 24:29–30. There His coming is described as accompanied by cosmic signs (24:29) and His glorious appearance in the sky (24:30). When that coming happens "then all the tribes of the earth will mourn, and they will see the Son of Man coming on the clouds of the sky with power and great glory" (24:30). The reason why the "tribes of the earth," that is the nations of the world will mourn is because He will come as a conqueror and judge. Revelation describes this coming.

> And I saw heaven opened, and behold, a white horse, and He who sat on it is called Faithful and True, and in righteousness He judges and wages war. His eyes are a flame of fire, and on His head are many diadems; and He has a name written on Him which no one knows except Himself. He is clothed with a robe dipped in blood, and His name is called The Word of God. And the armies which are in heaven, clothed in fine linen, white and clean, were following Him on white horses. From His mouth comes a sharp sword, so that with it He may strike down the nations, and He will rule them with a rod of iron; and He treads the wine press of the fierce wrath of God, the Almighty. (19:11–15)

This is the Second Coming as "King of kings and Lord of lords" (19:16). It is anything but peaceful and reassuring. When Jesus is speaking to His disciples in John 14, however, He is speaking of the rapture of the church. It is a coming for His own, to retrieve them, to take them to His Father's house. This will happen before He comes as conquering King and is an event most clearly pictured in First Thessalonians 4:13–18— very different from the event described in Matthew 24 and Revelation 19.

First Thessalonians 4:13–18

The preeminent passage on the rapture of the church and the resurrection of believers in the church age is First Thessalonians 4:13–18.

> But we do not want you to be uninformed, brethren, about those who are asleep, so that you will not grieve as do the rest who have no hope. For if we believe that Jesus died and rose again, even so God will bring with Him those who have fallen asleep in Jesus. For we say this to you by the word of the Lord, that we who are alive and remain until the coming of the Lord will not precede those who have fallen asleep. For the Lord Himself will descend from heaven with a shout, with the voice of the archangel and with the trumpet of God, and the dead in Christ will rise first. Then we who are alive and remain will be caught up together with them in the clouds to meet the Lord in the air, and so we will always be with the Lord. Therefore comfort one another with these words. (1 Thess. 4:13–18)

The account of how the apostle Paul had established the church in Thessalonica is recorded in Acts 17. Even though he and his companions were there only a few weeks ("three Sabbaths," Acts 17:2), Paul had taught them about the coming of the Lord Jesus Christ and other events to come in the "end times," and in his letters he refers to this teaching (2 Thess. 2:5) and to their knowledge of end-time events (1 Thess. 5:1–2).

After Paul hastily left Thessalonica (Acts 17:10), he moved on to preach the gospel in Berea (17:13) and went on to Athens (17:15); at that time he sent Timothy back to check on the church in Thessalonica (1 Thess. 3:1–2). Apparently during these travels of Paul and his entourage, some of the believers in Thessalonica had died, leading some to suppose that these believers had missed the Lord's return. In First Thessalonians 4:13–18 Paul corrects this misunderstanding.

Here Paul informs them about the gathering of the saints—the supernatural event of the "catching away" of the church. The death of loved ones and believers had opened the question of whether those believers missed that wonderful event?" It should be noted that Paul's purpose here was pastoral; he was not making an argument over rival views of the end times. He was informing the saints and comforting them so that they would not grieve the loss of loved ones as the world grieves (1 Thess. 4:13); believers are to have hope even at a time of loss. The ground of this hope is the death (securing an atonement; 1 Pet. 2:21–25; Isaiah 53) and resurrection of Jesus. Paul gave them the assurance they needed. He referred to these lost loved ones as being those who are asleep (used three times as a euphemism for death that gives the promise of an awakening). Those believers who are asleep in Jesus are not lost and gone forever but they are "with the Lord" (2 Cor. 5:8). This "sleep" pertained only to their bodies; they were otherwise conscious and in

His presence. This explains how these deceased ones can both return with Him (1 Thess. 4:14) and also rise first (4:16).

In First Thessalonians 4:15–17, Paul explains how the event of the "catching away" will unfold. There will be a series of distinctive happenings, and he introduces the details of the sequence by affirming that his teaching is grounded in the teaching of Christ; the Thessalonians can be confident of what Paul teaches since this is by the word of the Lord. (This may have in mind the teaching of Jesus in the so-called "Olivet Discourse" in Matthew chapters 24 and 25, or it indicate some traditional teaching of Jesus not preserved in the gospel record or Paul may have had some direct revelation otherwise unknown to posterity.)

At this point Paul delivers the most eloquent teaching on the "rapture" of the church to be found in the New Testament. He mentions the people involved, he details the main features of the event and he explains the point of his instruction. The term "rapture" comes from the Latin text of this passage which employs a form of the word *rapio* which means "to seize," or "to carry off violently."[2] This Latin term is used to translate the Greek term *harpazō* ("caught up") in First Thessalonians 4:17.

There are two groups of people involved. First, there are those who are "asleep in Jesus" (4:14), also recognized as "the dead in Christ" (4:16). These are those deceased believers whose fate and place in the eschatological program prompted this pastoral instruction. Second, there are the living believers who are identified twice as "we who are alive and remain" (4:15, 17). So Paul has in view here all who are New Testament believers, in Christ (4:16); that is, all Christians, members of the church, both deceased and living, will take part in this event. Furthermore, Paul emphasizes the point that the living church members are not given preferential treatment over the deceased. The loved ones of the Thessalonians who have died will not be left out, nor will they miss this great event. To the contrary, Christ will bring the living souls of those who died in Him to be reunited with their resurrected bodies (1 Cor. 15:51–58; see discussion later in this chapter). It is noteworthy that Paul includes himself with those who are alive and remain; he uses the personal pronoun "we"—"we who are alive and remain" (1 Thess. 4:15). This indicates that Paul believed the rapture could occur in his lifetime, and that it could occur at any time. This shows that Paul thought this was an imminent possibility—and it remains an imminent possibility to this day.

---

2 Alan Hultberg, "Introduction," *Three Views on the Rapture* (Grand Rapids, MI: Zondervan, 2020) 11.

Paul uses the name "Jesus," and the titles "Christ," and "Lord" to identify the One who is coming with ("will bring with Him," 1 Thess. 4:14) and for (to "be with the Lord," 4:17) the saints. It is emphatic that He Himself is the agent performing this work. This is in contrast to the event described in Matthew 24:31, where at the Second Coming the angels will "gather together His elect"—thus, there are two distinct events associated with the *parousia* (that is, the "Second Coming")—the rapture and the actual second coming (or "revelation") of Christ.[3]

The series of events attendant with the rapture of believers will commence when the Lord Himself descends from heaven (1 Thess. 4:16). At this time Paul informs the Thessalonians that there will be three distinct sounds. The first sound will be something like a "shout." The term here is used of a military command, or order which is authoritative, distinctive and intended to gain the attention of all who hear it. The second sound, Paul writes is "the voice of the archangel." The only archangel named in the Bible is Michael (Dan. 12:1–3; Jude 9), and in those texts his voice is not mentioned. The significance here seems to be that it will be like the shout of a commander—authoritative and distinctive—but also in some way it will be recognized as a supernatural sound or voice. This is to indicate the nature of this event—it is otherworldly and extraordinary. The third sound is the trumpet of God. The trumpet sound, as with the shout, has a military association to it and probably refers to a signaling or summoning purpose.

While the exact purpose or quality of these sounds is not stated by Paul, it seems likely that the purpose of these supernatural manifestations will be to summon believers and announce that the "blessed hope" (Titus 2:13) is about to be realized.

Next, Paul informed the Thessalonians that the souls of the dead in Christ will be reunited with their resurrected bodies when he writes, "the dead in Christ will rise first" (1 Thess. 4:16). As noted, at death the believer's immaterial nature (spirit) goes into the presence of the Lord consciously and enjoys that presence (see Phil. 1:21, 23). But this is not the

3 "Based on other texts that describe the Second Coming proper(Joel 2:12–16; Zech. 14:1–5; Rev. 19:11–21) there are significant differences between the two events: here [at the rapture] He comes in the air but then [Second Coming] He comes to the Mount of Olives; here the prospect is comfort and fellowship with the Lord, then the prospect is judgment (Matt. 24:36–41)." Much of this section is from Kevin D. Zuber, "1 Thessalonians," *The Moody Bible Commentary*, ed. by Michael Rydelnick and Michael Vanlaningham (Chicago: Moody Publishers, 2014), 1887–88.

end state of a believer in Christ. The Bible does not teach the immortality of the spirit apart from the body. It teaches the immortality of the entire person, body and spirit. Therefore, at the rapture of the church, the immaterial nature of believers will be joined once again to their resurrection bodies (see discussion later in this chapter on First Corinthians 15). They will spend eternity with the Lord Jesus Christ in this state. This effectively addressed the concerns of the Thessalonians; their loved ones will not miss the "blessed hope."

Paul next turned his attention to the living believers. He added himself to this group and affirmed, "Then we who are alive and remain will be caught up together with them" (1 Thess. 4:17); that is, living saints will join with those resurrected saints, in the experience of being "caught up." This event is described by the very expressive term "caught up" which (as noted previously) is the Greek term *harpazō*. This term means "snatch, seize, to take suddenly and vehemently, or to take away."[4] It describes "a strong, irresistible, even violent act."[5] In other places in the New Testament *harpazō* is used to describe a "taking by force," or "snatching away" (Matt. 11:12; John 10:12; Acts 8:39). This is not to suggest that this will be a violent or buffeting happening, or a frightening or terrorizing experience (in fact it will be quite the contrary!). But it will be sudden and irresistible.

The action of this event culminates "in the clouds" and "in the air" (1 Thess. 4:17). This is exactly what the angels told the disciples to expect in Acts 1 after Jesus had been "lifted up" and "a cloud received Him out of their sight" (Acts 1:9). When the disciples lingered "gazing intently into the sky" (1:10), the angels told them, "This Jesus, who has been taken up from you into heaven, will come in just the same way as you have watched Him go into heaven" (1:11). He departed by clouds into the sky—so He will come from heaven, and the saints will meet (*apantasis*) Him "in the clouds" and they will be with Him "in the air" (1 Thess. 4:17). Some hold that the term "to meet" (*apantasis*) has a technical meaning that points to a "visiting dignitary" who comes to the city and is met by an official delegation from the city.

---

4 See *A Greek-English Lexicon of the New Testament and Other Early Christian Literature, Second Edition*, edited by Walter Bauer, Wm. F. Arndt, and F. Wilbur Gingrich, revised by F. Wilbur Gingrich and Fredrick W. Danker (Chicago, IL: The University of Chicago Press, 1979) s.v. "ἁρπάζω," 109.

5 John MacArthur, *First & Second Thessalonians: MacArthur New Testament Commentary* (Chicago, IL: Moody Publishers, 202), 136.

After this meeting the dignitary and the delegation together return to the city. However, that idea is not supported by the use of "to meet" (*apantasis*) in secular Greek or in the two other uses of this term in the New Testament (Matt. 25:6, 10 in the parable of the ten virgins and in Acts 28:15 describing Paul's reception by the Christians in Rome).[6]

Paul simply notes that the outcome of this event will be that the saints "will always be with the Lord" (1 Thess. 4:17), which is the very hope of every believer—to be with Jesus forever.

First Corinthians 15

The Hope of the Believer: Bodily Resurrection

The hope of a Christian is not that of some Platonic realm of the ideals or forms, a purely spiritual disembodied existence divested of the debased and corrupted material world. The believer's hope is to follow his or her Lord Jesus Christ who is "the firstborn from the dead" (Col 1:18).

The most important chapter on the believer's hope of resurrection is found in First Corinthians 15. Here Paul presents his exposition in three parts. The believer's hope of resurrection is assured by the *fact of Christ's resurrection* (15:1–11). The believer's hope of resurrection is contrasted with the *folly of denying Christ's resurrection* (15:12–19). The believer's hope of resurrection, which is the focus of this section, is explained by the apostle Paul in First Corinthians 15:35–58. This text will be considered in several parts.

---

6 See Michael R. Crosby, "Hellenistic Formal Receptions and Paul's use of APANTHSIS in 1 Thessalonians 4:17," *Bulletin for Biblical Research* 4:1994, 19 [15–34]. Here, in effect, is a case of choosing between two metaphors to describe the event: either this is something like the "visiting dignitary" view wherein a group of city folk, officials and such, go out to greet an honored guest or conquering hero (and return to the city) or what is in view here is a Bridegroom, coming to retrieve His bride (in fulfillment of His promise—John 14:1–3) to take her to His Father's house where the wedding feast will complete the formal union of marriage (Rev. 9:7–9). The first view imports a metaphor that is not found anywhere else to describe Christ's relationship with His church (and in fact the text does not indicate that the Lord and the saints return to the city—it just says they are with Him always); the second view incorporates several other key texts and provides a richer explanation of the event, using a recognized metaphor—Bride/church and Bridegroom/Christ—from several other passages." This is mostly quoted from Kevin D. Zuber, "1 Thessalonians," *The Moody Bible Commentary*, ed. by Michael Rydelnick and Michael Vanlaningham (Chicago: Moody Publishers, 2014), 1887.

PAUL'S EXPOSITION ON THE RESURRECTION BODY

Part One: Different Bodies: First Corinthians 15:35–41

> But someone will say, "How are the dead raised? And with what kind of body do they come?" You fool! That which you sow does not come to life unless it dies; and that which you sow, you do not sow the body which is to be, but a bare grain, perhaps of wheat or of something else. But God gives it a body just as He wished, and to each of the seeds a body of its own. All flesh is not the same flesh, but there is one flesh of men, another flesh of beasts, another flesh of birds, and another of fish. There are also heavenly bodies and earthly bodies, but the glory of the heavenly is one, and the glory of the earthly is another. There is one glory of the sun, another glory of the moon, and another glory of the stars; for star differs from star in glory.

The questions with which this paragraph begins arise in the minds of the Corinthians because they were trying to reconcile their Greek (philosophically informed) worldview with the apostle Paul's teaching about the resurrection of Christ and of believers. Simply put, the Corinthians were steeped in a basically Platonic philosophical worldview that saw the realm of Plato's ideas or forms as the "real world" and the physical world of actual things as inferior copies of that ideal realm. In this philosophy the sensible world of physical matter, of tangible stuff, of corporeal bodies, was not merely inferior, but wrong—an error of a lesser being known as the *Demiurge*.[7] Humans beings (who have immortal spirits) were originally meant to live in that ideal world but have become stuck or stranded in physical bodies in this physical realm. The objective of a philosopher, thinker, or whoever was to find a way back up to the ideal world, to get out of this world of "chaos, change, and decay" and get back to that world of oneness with the "good" and harmony. This escape is made at death but is successful only if the individual is prepared for the transition from this lower physical realm to the higher ideal realm.

---

7 This term means something like "craftsman," or "artisan." The *Demiurge* as a proper noun for an entity (person) comes from Plato's dialogue *Timaeus*, written about 360 BC. In *Timaeus* the *Demiurge* is presented as the creator of the universe and in later Platonic thought this figure is said to be responsible for the physical realm. In other Greek philosophical systems he (or it) is either evil or his work of creation was so inferior it allowed evil to exist. In still other philosophical systems he (or it) is ignorant or was misguided. In any case, the creation of the physical world, according to the basically Platonic Greek philosophical worldview, was not a good thing and the Greek philosopher wanted to leave it and never return.

Given that worldview, the very idea that an enlightened person who has died would come back to life in a physical body was ludicrous! The Greek philosophical (Platonic) worldview of the Corinthians viewed this physical realm as a flawed, diminished, and even corrupted copy of the ideal world. In fact, to the Greek philosophical mind, this physical world was a mistake and the sooner one could leave it behind the better. To think of a return or resurrection back into this realm was the height of folly. (This is why "the Epicurean and Stoic philosophers" in Athens [Acts 17:18], who were listening to Paul's sermon on "the Areopagus" [or Mars Hill] scoffed at Paul. When Paul preached the resurrection of Jesus [17:31] Luke writes: "Now when they heard of the resurrection of the dead, some began to sneer" [17:32].) A physical, bodily resurrection made no sense to them, given their philosophical presuppositions. This is the very worldview that generated the questions of the Corinthians.

Paul's answer to those questions is given in two parts.

First, Paul uses a horticultural metaphor. When a farmer wants a crop he does not sow the final body but a seed. That seed must be planted—it must, in a sense, die. To get the plant (the body) that grows up from the seed, the seed must be transformed, in apparent death. No one is surprised to see wheat plants come from wheat seeds after those seeds are buried! And, Paul says, this is something that God (not the ideal world) inaugurated when He created this horticultural arrangement. Paul likely has Genesis 1:11 in mind here: "Then God said, 'Let the earth sprout vegetation, plants yielding seed, and fruit trees on the earth bearing fruit after their kind with seed in them'; and it was so." The two basic principles Paul is pointing to are the continuity of the seed-plant (they are both the same "wheat") and transformation (from "seed" body to another "body"). Paul does not explicitly make the application of this metaphor to the believer's resurrection just yet, but it is not difficult to see that he is undermining the presuppositions of the Corinthians' philosophical worldview. The seed is the source of the plant even though it "dies" and looks nothing like the "ideal" of the grown plant.

The second part of Paul's response to the questions of First Corinthians 15:35 likely continues to have Genesis 1 in mind. Here he observes that there are many different kinds of physical and fleshly bodies—men, animals, birds, fish. And, surprisingly, he contrasts these with "heavenly bodies"—the sun, moon, and stars. The point simply is, again, these bodies are all different, but they are suited to their realm (heavenly bodies fit in heaven and earthly bodies fit on earth). Furthermore, these bodies differ in glory. Again, Paul does not explicitly make the application of these comparisons, but the idea seems to be that if there is to be a resurrection of an earthly body it is expected to take on the "glory" that will allow it to "fit" the "heavenly realm."

In short, Paul is telling the Corinthians they needed to jettison their philosophical worldview and realize that God is the One who made the "heavenly realm" and the "earthly realm"; and He made the bodies that fit in each realm and the systems that operate in each realm; and, if He made the wheat seed that "dies" become a living wheat plant, He can transform the earthly body that dies into a body fit for the heavenly realm.

Part Two: Spiritual Bodies: First Corinthians 15:42–49

> So also is the resurrection of the dead. It is sown a perishable body, it is raised an imperishable body; it is sown in dishonor, it is raised in glory; it is sown in weakness, it is raised in power; it is sown a natural body, it is raised a spiritual body. If there is a natural body, there is also a spiritual body. So also it is written: "The first man, Adam, became a living soul." The last Adam became a life-giving spirit. However, the spiritual is not first, but the natural; then the spiritual. The first man is from the earth, earthy; the second man is from heaven. As is the earthy, so also are those who are earthy; and as is the heavenly, so also are those who are heavenly. Just as we have borne the image of the earthy, we will also bear the image of the heavenly.

It is here in these verses that Paul makes the application of the illustrations he gave in 15:35–41, as indicated by the phrase "So also is the resurrection of the dead" (15:42). As with the previous section, this section may also be divided into two parts.

First, Paul adds to the principles of continuity and transformation (which he alluded to in the metaphor of the seed-to-plant in 15:35–37). Like the seed which needed to "die," the believer's body is "sown a perishable body" (15:42). Paul continues the horticultural metaphor of the seed by using the word "sown" several times (15:42–44). It is interesting that even though he is speaking of the believer's body, he does not say buried. By doing this Paul anticipates that the outcome for the believer's body will be like the outcome for the seed—something will rise. Of course, unlike the seed which only seemed to die, the body of a deceased believer will decay and disintegrate. The expression "a perishable body" (Greek: *en phthora*) is literally "in corruption," or "in a state of decay," that is, deceased and decomposing. In the next two verses Paul adds to that description of the body of the deceased; it is sown in dishonor and weakness (15:43).

These terms refer to the deceased body with scorn, which is exactly how the Corinthians were thinking of the physical body from their Greek philosophical worldview. For them the body would have been disdained and regarded with condescension as a mere "natural body" (1 Cor. 15:44) even before death, but especially so after death. But Paul, using his seed metaphor, is letting the Corinthians know how wrong they were. What they and all believers must know is that for them death of the body is not a dismal, contemptuous end, but like a sowing of seed, it is buried with hope, expectation, and even anticipation. In the apostle Paul's masterful rhetorical flourish, the believer's body will be raised "imperishable," or *en aphthora*, "in incorruption" (notice the *a* added to *phthora*); it will be raised "in glory" and "in power," that is, it will not be at all what the Greek philosophers were thinking. It will be "a spiritual body" (15:44). This was a category the Corinthians, with their Greek philosophical worldview, had not considered, even though they should have, since they had the example of Christ's own risen and glorified body.

The word "spiritual" here in Greek is *pneumatikos*, and may have been the word the Corinthians used to describe their view of a "spiritual" non-bodily "resurrection." For Paul to, in effect, co-opt their term and use it along with the term for body (Greek: *sōma*)—hence *sōma pneumatikos*—would have been a stunning idea for the Corinthians, with their Greek philosophical worldview.[8] For these philosophically-minded Corinthians, those two—body and spirit—were two completely incommensurate states of existing—one contemptuous, one glorious. It would be like trying to imagine a beautiful and glorious, decaying lump of flesh. But, of course, what they were missing is the principle of transformation that takes place at the resurrection.

This is what the Corinthians needed to understand: The risen body of the believer will be:

1. *a real body*—not an ethereal, nebulous thing, like a hologram or an insubstantial, ghostly phantom;
2. *their own body*—like the wheat seed that grows into a wheat plant, there is continuity; but
3. *a transformed body*—just as earthy bodies of flesh (15:39) are made to "fit" the conditions of their existence, just so these *sōma pneumatikos* ("spiritual bodies") will be made to fit their new residence with the Lord (1 Thess. 4:17, "and so we shall always be with the Lord").

8 See Gordon D. Fee, The First Epistle to the Corinthians: The New International Commentary on the New Testament (Grand Rapids, MI: Eerdmans, 2014), 869.

In the second part of this section, Paul picks a comparison he had used earlier in First Corinthians 15:21–22: the contrast between Adam and Christ. In this contrast, the matter was death and life—the former became the representative head of the race (Adam) and the latter became the representative head of all who believe in Him, namely, Christ. Now, the contrast is between Adam—the "living soul" and Christ "the life-giving spirit."

Once again, Paul is thinking of Genesis, and he actually quotes a part of Gen. 2:7 when he says Adam "became a living soul" (1 Cor. 15:45). The point here is Adam became a "living being" and, in line with the thought of the entire chapter, Paul means that Adam had a "living body" (and again, that body was made to "fit" the creation God had completed). Adam's was a "natural body" (15:46); he was "from the earth" and his body was an "earthy body" (15:47); all who are the descendants of Adam "are earthy" and bear "the image of the earthy" (15:48–49). Christ by contrast is the "last Adam" and "the life-giving spirit" (based on the earlier contrast "in Christ all will be made alive.") When Paul refers to Christ as "the life-giving spirit" he is thinking of the new life that Christ inaugurated by His resurrection (Rom. 6:4; He is the "first fruits of those who are asleep," 1 Cor. 15:20). In contrast to Adam's natural body, Christ's body is "spiritual" and by this Paul is referring to Christ's resurrection body. Christ is "spiritual," (15:46) and "from heaven" (15:47). All who are "in Christ" (15:22) will bear the image of the heavenly" (15:49).

The key for Paul's point is verse 46, "the spiritual is not first, but the natural; then the spiritual" which looks back to verse 42. The entire contrast between Adam and Christ is about bodies, and is meant to let the Corinthians know that the sequence of "natural body first, then spiritual body" is the ordinary and obvious order. That being the case, they should not be disparaging the natural body (it was given by God!). In fact, there must be a natural "living body" before it can be transformed into a "spiritual body." Paul concludes, "Just as we have borne the image of the earthy, we will also bear the image of the heavenly" (15:49); which is to say the natural body, as it is in this earthy setting, is not the spiritual body believers will have in the heavenly realm. The thought here is summed up by the apostle Paul in Philippians where he assures them that the Lord Jesus Christ "will transform the body of our humble state into conformity with the body of His glory" (Phil. 3:21)

Part Three: Imperishable Bodies: First Corinthians 15:50–54

> Now I say this, brethren, that flesh and blood cannot inherit the kingdom of God; nor does the perishable inherit the imperishable. Behold, I tell you a mystery; we will not all sleep, but we will all be changed, in a moment, in the twinkling of an eye, at the last trumpet; for the trumpet will sound, and the dead will be raised imperishable, and we will be changed. For this perishable must put on the imperishable, and this mortal must put on immortality. But when this perishable will have put on the imperishable, and this mortal will have put on immortality, then will come about the saying that is written, "DEATH IS SWALLOWED UP in victory."

In this last section of his treatise on the believer's bodily resurrection, Paul describes the transformation he has been alluding to throughout the previous sections. He says very plainly that "flesh and blood cannot inherit the kingdom of God" (15:50). The Corinthians are wrong to characterize the resurrection in such crass physical terms in order to reject it. Paul admits, "nor does the perishable inherit the imperishable" (15:50), but he also affirms "this perishable must put on the imperishable" (15:53). Here again is the principle of transformation: "we will all be changed" (15:51). And yet it is "we," says Paul; it will still be "us" (in continuity); that is, "we" are the same persons who died ("the dead") who "will be raised imperishable" (15:52). These are the principles—continuity and transformation—that the Corinthians needed to know to transform their Greek philosophical worldview and correct their understanding about the bodily resurrection of believers. The body that is buried will be transformed and yet this transformed ("imperishable") body has continuity with the body ("perishable") that was "sown" (or buried). This—continuity and transformation—is the hope of the believer.

How transformation happens is something of a mystery, but Paul says it will be sudden ("in a moment, in the twinkling of an eye," 15:52). It will be dramatic and it will be definitive.

It is the apostle John who gives a bit more information about this change: "Beloved, now we are children of God, and it has not appeared as yet what we will be. We know that when He appears, we will be like Him, because we will see Him just as He is" (1 John 3:2). In other words, that transformation that will come at the resurrection will be into "the image of the heavenly" One—Jesus Christ (1 Cor. 15:49). This promise should motivate believers to live pure and Christlike lives, for as John writes, "everyone who has this hope fixed on Him purifies himself, just as He is pure" (1 John 3:3).

What does the Bible say about Cremation? Should Christians be Cremated?

This is a question that regularly arises in most discussions about the believer's hope of bodily resurrection. The concern is obvious; if a believer dies in hope of the bodily resurrection, is it then appropriate to want his or her body to be cremated? Would that not imply an implicit denial of that hope?

Several points must be established to address this question. First, it must be admitted that the Bible is relatively silent on this matter. For the authors of Scripture, this does not seem to be an issue. There were instances of persons being burned to death (1 Kings 16:18—in this instance, in an act of suicide; 2 Kings 21:6—in this instance, associated with pagan worship practices). Also, there is the instance of Josiah having the bones of the deceased idolatrous priests burned on the altar where they had made their idolatrous sacrifices in order to "defile it" and make it unusable thereafter (2 Kings 23:15–16). The actions associated with the burning of the body (suicide, pagan worship) are to be condemned, to be sure; but these are not instances of cremation as a normal burial practice, and so they do not speak to the question of the propriety of cremation.

The actual burning of bodies intentionally was rare and usually happened only as a judgment when there was a serious violation of the Word of the Lord, as in the case of Achan, who had violated the ban on taking the spoil of Jericho (Josh. 7:15, 25; Lev. 20:14; 21:9). The burning of the bodies of Saul and his sons by the men of Jabeh-gilead (1 Sam. 31:12) should be taken as an isolated incident, and may actually have been done out of respect for the deceased whose bodies had been disrespected by the Philistines (31:10). This can be seen by the respectful and dignified burial of their bones (31:13).

In the New Testament the several references to deceased believers as "being asleep" makes it appear that the practice of intentional cremation would have seemed inappropriate to most believers in the early church. The early church, accordingly, preferred burial of the body—following the pattern of Jesus' burial—in hope of the resurrection. Many early martyrs were burned at the stake and yet there is no evidence that this undermined the church's faith in the bodily resurrection, and it was not regarded as something that would mitigate their hope of resurrection. It is recorded in the *Martyrdom of Polycarp* (18:2) that after the martyr was burned, the ashes were collected and buried, giving evidence that though the body had been burned, this did not affect the believer's hope of the resurrection of the martyr.[9]

Cremation has been practiced by many cultures for thousands of years and at times, it has been associated with religious practices. Cremation is the preferred burial practice for Hinduism and Buddhism and other eastern religions, and that association has led many Christian denominations to frown on it. Some cultures and religions are strongly opposed to the practice (Islam for instance), and others do not consider it a standard or generally acceptable practice (Judaism for instance).

Whether cremation is chosen or not, it should be emphasized that, cremated or buried, the believer's hope of bodily resurrection is assured. It has been noted by many that most of the bodies of believer's that were buried over the centuries have decayed and turned to dust, and yet their hope of bodily resurrection is as certain today as when their physical bodies were placed in the grave. God is all-powerful, the Creator of bodies and the Giver of life. He is just as able to raise the body of a believer who has been cremated as He is to raise the body of a believer that was buried, has decayed, and turned to dust. Thus, it seems best to consider the question of cremation or burial as a matter of Christian freedom.[10]

---

9 G. A. Turner, "Cremation," in The International Standard Bible Encyclopedia Vol. One: A-D, Revised, ed. by Geoffrey W. Bromiley, Everett F. Harrison, Roland Harrison, William Sanford LaSor (Grand Rapids, MI: Eerdmans, 1979), 813.

10 For more information on the matter of cremation see John J. Davis, *What About Cremation?: A Christian Perspective* (Winona Lake, IN: Pinegrove Publishing, 1998).

Study Questions:

1. What is the meaning of the Greek term *elpizō* and how does that distinguish the world's view of hope?

2. What was the concern of the Thessalonians that prompted the apostle Paul to write First Thessalonians 4:13–18?

3. What are the parts of the series of distinctive happenings by which the apostle Paul describes how the event of the "catching away" will unfold?

4. What is the meaning of the Greek term *harpazō*?

5. What is the meaning of the Greek term "to meet" (*apantasis*)?

6. What is the problem with the Greek (philosophically informed) worldview of the Corinthians that prompted the apostle Paul to write First Corinthians 15?

7. What is the metaphor the apostle Paul uses in First Corinthians 15:42–49 to describe the resurrection?

8. How do the principles of continuity and transformation apply to explain the resurrection?

9. Does the Bible reject the practice of cremation?

11

Heaven

THE ENGLISH WORD "heaven" is found about six hundred times in Scripture and is used to translate the Hebrew *shamayim* ("the heights") and the Greek term *ouranos* ("something raised up or lofty"). But in order to discuss heaven, we have to agree on some terms.

The Several Meanings of "Heaven"

When the Bible refers to "heaven," or "the heavens" it has one of three places in view: the nearest heaven is the atmospheric heavens; beyond that are the planetary or cosmic heavens (the sun, moon, and stars); and beyond that is the transcendent or third heaven (2 Cor. 12:2). Sometimes these are referred to as the first, second, and third heaven, but only the last of these uses the ordinal number and is actually called the "third" heaven in Scripture.

The so-called "first heaven" is the atmosphere that surrounds the surface of the earth. While the atmosphere of breathable air is found from sea-level to the troposphere, the references to this "heaven" usually point to the clouds from which rain falls (Gen. 7:11–12; Ps. 147:8; Acts 14:17).

The "second heaven" is the sphere where the sun, moon, and stars move in their constant and regular courses. It is this constancy and regularity which allows these heavenly bodies to do the service for which they were created—namely "to rule the day and . . . to rule the night" (Gen. 1:16). These heavenly bodies were created to provide the earth with a cosmic clock and calendar, and to "be for signs and for seasons and for days and years" (1:14). And of course, "God placed them in the expanse of the heavens to give light on the earth" (1:17). These bodies, as they run their courses were also intended to reveal the glory of God (Ps. 19:1–4).

The "third heaven" is identified as such by the apostle Paul in Second Corinthians 12:2. In a later verse, he also cryptically refers to the place as "Paradise," where he was caught up and "heard inexpressible" revelations (12:4). It is this "third heaven" that is the focus of this study.

The Place of God's Dwelling, Throne, and Authority

Heaven is where God is; which is why Jesus taught His disciples to pray "Our Father who is in heaven" (Matt. 6:9). Jesus used the expression "your Father who is in heaven" a number of times (Matt. 5:16, 45; 6:1; 7:11; 18:14) and likewise the expression, "My Father who is in heaven" (7:21; 10:32–33; 12:50; 16:17; 18:10, 19). Of course, God is omnipresent (Ps. 139:7–10) and He fills the universe (Jer. 23:24), but His residence ("My Father's house," John 14:2) is in heaven. Heaven is the place where God is said to dwell (1 Kings 8:30). God's presence in heaven is a unique presence, where He manifests, or displays His being, as He does nowhere else (Isa. 6:1–9).

The association of "heaven" with the presence of God led to using the term "heaven" as virtually a synonym for God as when Jesus asked the Pharisees about the source of John the Baptist's authority to baptize: "The baptism of John was from what source, from heaven or from men?" (Matt. 21:25). Here "heaven" refers to God, as it does when John himself said, "A man can receive nothing unless it has been given him from heaven" (John 3:27). When the prodigal son confessed his sin to his father in these terms, "I have sinned against heaven and in your sight" (Luke 15:21), he meant "I have sinned against God and you."

Scripture often speaks in terms of "heaven above" and "earth beneath" as in Psalm 103:11, "For as high as the heavens are above the earth" (see also Isa. 55:9). Psalm 53:2 says, "God has looked down from heaven" (see also 14:2) and Psalm 33:13 says, "The Lord looks from heaven." These texts view heaven as a place "high above" the earth, in the sense that it is "transcendent"—a higher plane of existence.

Heaven is where God's throne is, the place from which He exercises His rule and reign over the earth. In Psalm 11:4, David declares, "The Lord is in His holy temple; the Lord's throne is in heaven." In Revelation 4:2, John saw that "a throne was standing in heaven, and One sitting on the throne." This is very much the same vision as Isaiah (Isa. 6:1–9), for John says he saw around the throne those who were continually saying, "Holy, holy, holy is the Lord God, the Almighty" (Rev. 4:8). In Isaiah 66:1, the Lord Himself affirms, "Heaven is My throne and the earth is My footstool" (see also Acts 7:49). In Psalm 2:4, the psalmist reveals that God the Father "sits in the heavens" and "laughs" at the rebellious nations on His footstool, the earth, who challenge His authority.

God hears the prayers of His people in heaven. In Second Chronicles 7:14, He promised His people that if they would "humble themselves and pray and seek My face and turn from their wicked ways, then I will hear from heaven, will forgive their sin and will heal their land." Likewise, in Nehemiah 9:27, the Levite worship leaders (9:5) recalled the time when the people "cried to You in the time of their distress" and the LORD "heard from heaven" and answered those prayers "according to [His] great compassion." This indicates that while heaven is "above" and "transcendent," it is not a place so wholly removed from the earth that God cannot see and hear His people.

The Place Jesus Ascended to and from which He Will Return

Hebrews 9:24 states that Christ has entered into heaven and is serving in His high priestly ministry of intersession on our behalf (Rom. 8:34; Heb. 7:25). This was what Jesus Himself anticipated when He spoke of returning to His Father: "I came forth from the Father and have come into the world; I am leaving the world again and going to the Father" (John 16:28). When Mary Magdalene saw the risen Lord Jesus, she embraced Him, but Jesus gently commanded her, "Stop clinging to Me," because He said, "I have not yet ascended to the Father" (20:17). He then instructed her to "go to My brethren and say to them, 'I ascend to My Father and your Father, and My God and your God.'" This ascension took place forty days after His resurrection (Acts 1:3), in full view of His disciples. Luke described the scene in these words in Acts 1: "And after He had said these things, He was lifted up while they were looking on, and a cloud received Him out of their sight" (1:9). This cloud was likely both a real cloud of water vapor in the sky, and also a supernatural cloud that appears several times in the Bible as a manifestation of the presence of God (Exod. 13:21–22; 24:16–18; 40:34–38; Num. 9:15–23; this cloud is called the *Shekinah* glory and visibly depicts the presence of the invisible God).

When Jesus ascended, He entered the presence of God and His glory in heaven. This is made clear, as Luke's record of Jesus' ascension continued, "And as they were gazing intently into the sky while He was going, behold, two men in white clothing stood beside them" (Acts 1:10). These were no doubt angels and they spoke to the disciples, "'Men of Galilee, why do you stand looking into the sky? This Jesus, who has been taken up from you into heaven, will come in just the same way as you have watched Him go into heaven'" (1:11). Having ascended Jesus returned to the glory He had prayed for in John 17:5: "Now, Father, glorify Me together with Yourself, with the glory which I had with You before the world was."

The word of the angels assured the disciples that Jesus will return "in just the same way as you have watched Him go" (Acts 1:11); that is, He will return to earth from this heaven in the clouds (Dan. 7:13; 1 Thess. 4:17). Jesus ascended to heaven in a literal—even if risen and glorified—body and He will return from heaven in that same risen and glorified body (Matt. 24:30).

THE NATURE OF HEAVEN

A Holy, Glorious Habitation of God

Because it is the place where God's presence is, heaven is a holy and glorious place. In Deuteronomy 26:15, the people are instructed to pray to the LORD, "Look down from Your holy habitation, from heaven, and bless Your people Israel," and David assures the people of God, "He will answer him from His holy heaven" (Ps. 20:6). Isaiah recorded the words of the LORD, "the high and exalted One Who lives forever, whose name is Holy" and He declared, "I dwell on a high and holy place." But this lofty, holy, heavenly dwelling does not remove Him from His people for He added, "And also with the contrite and lowly of spirit / In order to revive the spirit of the lowly / And to revive the heart of the contrite" (Isa. 57:15).

In His high-priestly prayer, Jesus prayed for His return to heavenly glory: "Now, Father, glorify Me together with Yourself, with the glory which I had with You before the world was" (John 17:5). The Lord Jesus will come from heaven "in His glory" and "He will sit on His glorious throne" (Matt. 25:31; Mark 8:38).

A Paradise for Believers

From the cross Jesus reassured the repentant thief, "Truly I say to you, today you shall be with Me in Paradise" (Luke 23:43). Paul told the Corinthians that he was "caught up into Paradise" (2 Cor. 12:4). In that same context he says this was being "caught up to the third heaven" (12:2). The only other use of this term (Greek *paradeisos*) is in Revelation 2:7, where the Risen Lord Jesus Christ promises, "To him who overcomes, I will grant to eat of the tree of life which is in the Paradise of God." The reference here to the "tree of life" recalls the tree in the Garden of Eden, which is fitting since the word "paradise" is a Persian loan word that means "a garden," or "a park." In each of these uses the term "paradise" is simply another refence to heaven and depicts heaven as a pleasant place of serenity and peace. Thus, Jesus' promise in Revelation 2:7 is that the believer will partake of the "tree of life" and enjoy "eternal life" in heaven, a place of tranquility and quiet rest.

What Is There for Believers in Heaven?

Glorification!

When believers reach heaven, they will have experienced the final phase of their salvation. The salvation of believers starts with regeneration, which is when the Holy Spirit causes one to be born again (1 Pet. 1:3), imparts new life and one is given the gift of faith (Eph. 2:5, 8). That one becomes a new creation (2 Cor. 5:17; Eph. 4:24), receives a new nature (2 Pet. 1:4), and enters into a new relationship with God (John 1:12). After regeneration one is a believer and begins the process of sanctification, in which the believer is "set apart," from sin (Col 3:5–9; 1 Pet. 1:14–15), from the world (1 John 2:15) and to God (1 Thess. 1:9). Sanctification is also progress in holiness (2 Cor. 7:1) and a growing into the conformity of Christlikeness (2 Pet. 3:18). The final phase of the believer's salvation is glorification, which is when he or she will be fully "conformed to the image of His Son" (Rom. 8:29; 1 John 3:3), and actually made holy as He is holy (1 Pet. 1:16).

The believer will have no sin in heaven! The struggle with sin, so graphically described by the apostle Paul in Romans 7 will be finally and fully at an end! Paul's cry "Who will set me free from the body of this death?" will be answered once and for all—"we will be like Him" (1 John 3:2).

What Will Heaven Be Like?[1]

In heaven believers will know maximum joy. In Psalm 16, after David expresses his assurance of his resurrection, he speaks of his expectation for what comes next, namely, to be with the Lord, "In Your presence is fullness of joy; / In Your right hand there are pleasures forever" (Ps. 16:11). In God's presence there will be inexpressible joy and eternal delight.

In heaven believers will have compete knowledge. Paul acknowledges, "For now we see in a mirror dimly," but his expectation is that in heaven we shall know God "face to face; now I know in part, but then I will know fully just as I also have been fully known" (1 Cor. 13:12). This does not mean that believers will be omniscient like God, but that the doubts and confusion that

1 The points of outline and thoughts for this section are drawn from John MacArthur, *The Glory of Heaven: The Truth About Heaven Angels and Eternal Life*, Second Edition (Wheaton, IL: Crossway, 2013), chapter 7, 130–155.

arise from their lack of a thorough knowledge of God's word, or the effects of sin and worldliness on their thinking will be removed so that they will be able to think God's thoughts after Him fully and consistently.

In heaven believers will know perfect comfort and rest. The Bible has much to say on the subject of rest. The Lord rested on the seventh day after creation (Gen. 2:3) as an example and pattern for the Sabbath rest which He intended for His people (Exod. 20:8). Though men desire peace and rest, Isaiah wrote "But the wicked are like the tossing sea, For it cannot be quiet, And its waters toss up refuse and mud. 'There is no peace,' says my God, 'for the wicked'" (Isa. 57:20–21). Jesus called those who desired rest to Himself, "Come to Me, all who are weary and heavy-laden, and I will give you rest. Take My yoke upon you and learn from Me, for I am gentle and humble in heart, and you will find rest for your souls" (Matt. 11:28–29). But the lasting rest He spoke of is yet future: "So there remains a Sabbath rest for the people of God" (Heb. 4:9) and the author of Hebrews encouraged his readers to "be diligent to enter that rest" (4:11).

The desire for rest in this life is never satisfied. But the promise—as for the tribulation saints in Revelation 14, so for all believers—is, "'Blessed are the dead who die in the Lord from now on!' 'Yes,' says the Spirit, 'so that they may rest from their labors, for their deeds follow with them'" (Rev. 14:13).

In heaven believers will know the fulfillment of all for which they hoped. In Romans 8 the apostle Paul reminded the Romans of their hope, "For in hope we have been saved, but hope that is seen is not hope; for who hopes for what he already sees? But if we hope for what we do not see, with perseverance we wait eagerly for it" (Rom. 8:24–25). It is in heaven that the hope will be realized because "hope does not disappoint" (Rom. 5:5).

In heaven believers will be reunited with loved ones who know the Lord. That believers will know one another according to their earthly identities may be concluded from the fact that at the transfiguration Peter and the others recognized Moses and Elijah and called them by name (Matt. 17:4). Jesus also affirmed that the patriarchs are still identified by the names Abraham, Isaac, and Jacob (22:32). At the last supper Jesus promised the disciples that He would drink the cup with them "when I drink it new with you in My Father's kingdom" (26:29), indicating they would know and recognize each other then. And when Paul speaks of the rapture of the church (1 Thess. 4:13–18), he describes a reunion with those who had "fallen asleep" and this seems to give a reason to think that those believers—those living and those raised—will know each other. The reunion with loved ones who know Christ, who have died and are now with the Lord (2 Cor. 5:8) is one of the most precious of all promises of heaven.

Like Angels?

In Matt. 22:30, Jesus makes the observation that believers will be "like angels." This does not mean believers will actually become angels. (The whole notion that believers will "get their wings" or do good deeds on earth as angels comes from the biblically uninformed imagination of Hollywood writers and movie makers. Nothing like this is even hinted in Scripture!)

Also, this does not necessarily mean that in heaven believers will not be related to their loved ones anymore. The point that Jesus is making is that there will be no procreation in heaven, no raising of children, no need for mothers to nurture children or for fathers to provide for the family. Those roles will be unnecessary. But there is no reason to think our closest earthly relationships will be entirely dissolved; in heaven those relationships may not be exactly the same, but we will know our loved ones—and that will not be in a lesser way but in a way exceedingly more joyful, rich, and meaningful than we have on earth.

THE JOYS OF HEAVEN

Heaven itself will be an unimaginable blessing and reward. But being in heaven will afford the believer many blessings beside that of just being there.

Christ in Heaven

The believer will be with Christ in heaven and will be glorified with Christ, (Rom. 8:17–18; Phil. 3:21; Col 3:4; 1 John 3:2). They will be "heirs also, heirs of God and fellow heirs with Christ" (Rom. 8:17). Peter also mentions this inheritance and describes it as "an inheritance which is imperishable and undefiled and will not fade away, reserved in heaven" (1 Pet. 1:4). The believer "will also live with Him" and "will also reign with Him" (2 Tim. 2:11–12; Rev. 3:21; 5:10; 20:4; 22:5). Along with that service the believer will sit in judgment with Christ (Dan. 7:22; Matt. 19:28; Luke 22:30; 1 Cor. 6:2).

Life in Heaven

The believer will know the full meaning and blessing of eternal life (Luke 18:30; John 6:40; 17:2–3; Rom. 2:7; 6:23; 1 John 5:11). The believer will experience an eternal weight of glory (2 Cor. 4:17). The believer will be as shining as the stars (Dan. 12:3). The believer "will have the Lord for an everlasting light, And your God for [their] glory" (Isa. 60:19). The believer will have a "house" (new and glorified body) eternal in the heavens (2 Cor. 5:1) and live in a kingdom (Matt. 25:34; Luke 22:29; Heb. 12:28). The ultimate heavenly home of believers will be the New Jerusalem, which is described as a place with incredibly beautiful gem stones ("Her brilliance was like a very costly stone, as a stone of crystal-clear jasper," Rev. 21:11) and precious metals ("and the city was pure gold, like clear glass," 21:18). John's full description is stunning:

> The foundation stones of the city wall were decorated with every kind of precious stone. The first foundation stone was jasper; the second, sapphire; the third, chalcedony; the fourth, emerald; the fifth, sardonyx; the sixth, sardius; the seventh, chrysolite; the eighth, beryl; the ninth, topaz; the tenth, chrysoprase; the eleventh, jacinth; the twelfth, amethyst. And the twelve gates were twelve pearls; each one of the gates was a single pearl. And the street of the city was pure gold, like transparent glass. (Rev. 21:19–21)

Actually, the joys of life in heaven are indescribable (1 Cor. 2:9) and anything good thing or spiritual blessing that believers experience now is only a taste "of the heavenly gift" (Heb. 6:4).

Eternal Worship in Heaven

One of the most important obligations of the believer, which is at the same time one of his or her greatest joys is the worship of God. Many Psalms exhort believers to worship—to cite just one "Exalt the Lord our God, / And worship at His footstool; / Holy is He" (Ps. 99:5). Jesus instructed the Samaritan woman (in John 4) that "those who worship Him must worship in spirit and truth" (John 4:24). Indeed, He told her "the true worshipers will worship the Father in spirit and truth; for such people the Father seeks to be His worshipers" (4:23). The problem is that much while believers are on earth much worship is insincere and unacceptable to God (Isa. 1:12–15). And like all things, even for believers, worship—as wonderful as it is a times—is done with mixed motives and is interrupted by the other obligations of life.

But the worship of heaven will be uninterrupted and always pure and performed with unmixed sincerity. John describes the worship of the tribulation saints in heaven who worship "before the throne of God; and they serve Him day and night in His temple" (Rev. 7:15). They will follow the pattern of the "four living creatures" who "day and night" "do not cease" in their praise of God Almighty (Rev. 4:8). This is what worship will be like for all the saints when they are all together in heaven.

Eternal Fellowship with God in Heaven

Along with worship one of the greatest joys of heaven will be the inestimable blessing of eternal fellowship with God. David expresses the desire that all believers have (or should have) in this life in Ps. 63:1, "O God, You are my God; I shall seek You earnestly; My soul thirsts for You, my flesh yearns for You, In a dry and weary land where there is no water." And the psalmist Asaph echoed that desire when he wrote of God, "besides You, I desire nothing on earth" (Ps. 73:25). But Asaph elevated his thought when he wrote "Whom have I in heaven but You?" (73:25). The fellowship with God in heaven is what theologians in previous times called "the beatific vision"—the face-to-face communion with God which all believers long for (1 John 3:2).

Believers in Christ have a sense of that fellowship even now, as Paul reminded the Corinthians "God is faithful, through whom you were called into fellowship with His Son, Jesus Christ our Lord" (1 Cor. 1:9). Also, the apostle John wrote that even now "indeed our fellowship is with the Father, and with His Son Jesus Christ" (1 John 1:3). And yet this desire for fellowship with God is never fully satisfied in this life, and the temporal communion with God believers enjoy is never lasting and cannot be, due to our flesh and weakness (Matt. 26:41).

That is why believers long for heaven where that fellowship will be full, satisfying, unbroken, and everlasting. That promise is found in Rev. 21:3: "Behold, the tabernacle of God is among men, and He will dwell among them, and they shall be His people, and God Himself will be among them." "That verse emphasizes God's intimate presence 'with man'—among humanity. The idea is that God himself will pitch his tent among the redeemed of the human race and make his dwelling among them. All believers will forever enjoy the pleasure of God's company."[2]

WHAT WILL NOT BE IN HEAVEN

A wonderful part of the experience of the believer in heaven will be about what is not there! There will be no sin or unrighteousness in heaven. The apostle Paul assured the Corinthians "that the unrighteous will not inherit the kingdom of God . . . [for] neither fornicators, nor idolaters, nor adulterers, nor effeminate, nor homosexuals, nor thieves, nor the covetous, nor drunkards, nor revilers, nor swindlers, will inherit the kingdom of God" (1 Cor. 6:9–10). Paul did not mean that anyone who had ever sinned in these ways

2 MacArthur, ,*The Glory of Heaven*, 153.

was excluded from the kingdom, for he went on to say to the Corinthians, "Such were some of you" (6:11). They had been involved in those sins, but they had been saved, "washed . . . sanctified, [and] . . . justified in the name of the Lord Jesus Christ and in the Spirit of our God" (6:11). The point here is that no one in heaven will be involved in those sins anymore! In the apostle John's vision of the New Jerusalem (Rev. 21:1–2) he assures his readers "and nothing unclean, and no one who practices abomination and lying, shall ever come into it" (21:27). That is because all "the cowardly and unbelieving and abominable and murderers and immoral persons and sorcerers and idolaters and all liars, their part will be in the lake that burns with fire and brimstone, which is the second death" (21:8). In the New Jerusalem (and so also in heaven), will be "only those whose names are written in the Lamb's book of life" (21:27), that is those who have been cleansed and redeemed by the blood of Christ (Matt. 26:28; Eph. 1:7; Heb. 9:22; 1 John 1:7, 9). In heaven believers will not be tempted to sin, they will not practice sin, they will not fall into sin, and they will not have to deal with the sins of others!

There Will Be Neither Sorrow nor Tears in Heaven

Whereas life on earth is often hard, and the necessities of life occupy so much attention and effort and even struggle, in heaven the believers will rest and "they will hunger no longer, nor thirst anymore; nor will the sun beat down on them, nor any heat" (Rev. 7:16).

Again in the apostle John's vision of the New Jerusalem, there is a very precious promise: "and He will wipe away every tear from their eyes; and there will no longer be any death; there will no longer be any mourning, or crying, or pain (21:4). One passage says that the Lamb will "wipe every tear from their eyes" (7:17), but this does not mean that believers will initially be weeping in heaven. It means that there will not be "anything to be sorry about—no sadness, no disappointment, no pain. There will be no tears of misfortune, tears over lost love, tears of remorse, tears of regret, tears over the death of loved ones, or tears for any other reason."[3]

There Will Be No Curse and No Darkness in Heaven

The apostle John makes this explicit: "There will no longer be any curse; and the throne of God and of the Lamb will be in it, and His bond-servants will serve Him; they will see His face, and His name will be on their foreheads.

3 John MacArthur, Revelation 12–22: *The MacArthur New Testament Commentary* (Chicago, IL: Moody Press, 2000), 269.

And there will no longer be any night; and they will not have need of the light of a lamp nor the light of the sun, because the Lord God will illumine them; and they will reign forever and ever" (Rev. 22:3–5).

THE REWARDS OF THE BELIEVER

The believer's expectation of heaven includes rewards. It is surprising to some that with all the glories of heaven and fellowship with Christ, that there will also be rewards. It has been asked, "Isn't Jesus enough?" But since Scripture speaks of rewards, it is appropriate that these rewards be understood.

The Believer's Crowns of Reward

In addition to the general rewards and blessings of heaven, a believer can look forward to some particular rewards which Scripture calls "crowns." The Greek word translated "crown" is *stephanos* (from which comes the name "Stephen," which was the name of the first martyr of the church, Acts 7). The noun *stephanos* comes from the verb *stepho*, meaning "to encircle," thus *stephanos* means "that which surrounds," and from that it refers to a garland, or wreath which was often made of a twig or branch of a tree or some other plant which was twisted into a circle. Such a *stephanos* was the victor's wreath or crown which was worn on the head and was awarded to the winner of an athletic contest in the games such as Olympic-type games. It is seldom used to refer to the crown of royalty or authority. At times a festive garland (*stephanos*) would be worn by important guests at a wedding or by noble attenders to the coronation of a king. Typically, it was viewed as an award or honor for some outstanding accomplishment or service. Thus, this term is used to refer to the rewards which God will bestow in heaven to believers who had been diligent and faithful in life. The crowns of reward mentioned in the New Testament are: the imperishable crown (1 Cor. 9:24–25), the crown of rejoicing (1 Thess. 2:19), the crown of righteousness (2 Tim. 4:8), the crown of glory (1 Pet. 5:4), and the crown of life (Rev. 2:10).

The imperishable crown is mentioned in First Corinthians 9:24–25): "Do you not know that those who run in a race all run, but only one receives the prize? Run in such a way that you may win. Everyone who competes in the games exercises self-control in all things. They then do it to receive a perishable wreath, but we an imperishable." Here Paul makes explicit the analogy between the *stephanos* of the winner of an athletic contest and the *stephanos* to be given to believers who "Run in such a way that [they] may win." Paul implicitly draws attention to the self-control that is part of the training and effort expended by athletes to get a mere wreath or garland of twigs and leaves. Of course, that "perishable wreath" accorded the victor a momentary acclaim, but it was a fleeting, fading honor. Every athlete knows he or she will be beaten one day!

In the era of the Roman empire, when a Roman general had won a great military victory, he would be given a "triumph"—a parade of honor through the streets of Rome. He would ride in a chariot followed by his family and associates, who were in turn followed by his defeated enemies in chains. It was a tremendous honor. However, in the chariot with him was a slave, holding a wreath, like a *stephanos*, over his head and this slave would keep repeating the phrase *omnis gloria fluxa*—"all glory is fleeting." That is something of Paul's point about the crown of the runner in those ancient games—the crown, and the honor, would wither and fade.

On the other hand, the *stephanos* to be awarded to the believer, Paul says, is an imperishable *stephanos*. The Greek term *phthartos* means "corruptible," "subject to decay"; the term here adds an "a" to that term to negate the meaning, thus *aphthartos* means "incorruptible," "not subject to decay." Paul does not spell out the application here but the point seems to be self-evident. If athletes put so much effort, and self-discipline, and focus to win a mere wreath of twigs and leaves, how much more effort, self-discipline, and focus should believers expend to run their race in this life, knowing they will receive a *stephanos*, with its undiminishing honor? What is this honor? The faithful believers will be honored in heaven simply by their presence there, which will afford them the eternal honor and joy of fellowship with God in Christ, and eternal worship of their Lord.

Paul calls this reward a *crown of rejoicing* : "For who is our hope or joy or crown of exultation? Is it not even you, in the presence of our Lord Jesus at His coming? For you are our glory and joy" (1 Thess. 2:19–20). Here the reward is the joy of relationships with other believers in heaven. Perhaps this refers to the very ones that believers themselves have led to Christ. Paul looked forward to Christ's coming and the "crowning joy" would be to see the Thessalonians there with him in heaven with Christ. More generally this is the joy of being in heaven with untold numbers of other faithful believers who lived for and served Christ over centuries.

Paul calls this reward a *crown of righteousness*: "In the future there is laid up for me the crown of righteousness, which the Lord, the righteous Judge, will award to me on that day; and not only to me, but also to all who have loved His appearing" (2 Tim. 4:8). When the apostle Paul says this crown is "laid up," he means it is safely and securely stored in heaven. Jesus referred to this secure storage when He encouraged His disciples, "But store up for yourselves treasures in heaven, where neither moth nor rust destroys, and where thieves do not break in or steal; for where your treasure is, there your heart will be also" (Matt. 6:20–21). And Paul wrote to Timothy that he needed to instruct the saints he was shepherding to store "up for themselves the treasure of a good foundation for the future" (1 Tim. 6:19). There are "treasures" in heaven, but they are not wealth, houses, or any physical possession, but lasting peace, unending joy, fulfilling and mutually enriching relationships (see previously under the crown of rejoicing), and mostly the presence of God.

This *stephanos* is "the crown of righteousness"—which is not the crown that comes from being righteous but the crown which is righteousness. This is the righteous received by faith, the justification given as a gift (Rom. 3:24).[4] This righteousness is a legal declaration by God, an imputation (reckoning) of God, for all those who put their full faith in the sin-covering, debt-paying sacrifice of Jesus Christ, which says, in effect, that they stand before God as righteous. This is not their own righteousness (which is really no righteousness at all [Isa. 64:6; Phil. 3:9]), but Christ's righteousness, which is counted to them by God and received by them by faith (Rom. 3:26, 28).

Here Paul is speaking of "the crown of eternal righteousness—the very righteousness of the Redeemer granted in full perfection to the glorified believer."[5] In effect, this is referring to the believer's glorification. This crown is the culminating, symbolic, and final proof of the imputed righteousness given to all believers, "all who have loved His appearing."

The crown of glory is mentioned in First Peter 5:4: "And when the Chief Shepherd appears, you will receive the unfading crown of glory." Since in the context of this verse Peter is writing to elders or pastors (5:1), some think this crown is reserved for elders or pastors alone. Others see this crown as another reference to the crown of righteousness, because it seems quite

4 "Justification is a legal pronouncement made by God in the present, prior to the day of judgment, declaring sinners to be not guilty and therefore to be acquitted, by pardoning all their sins and reckoning them to be righteous in His sight, on the basis of Christ as their representative and substitute, whose righteousness in life and death is put to their account when in self-despairing trust they look to Him alone for salvation." Philip H. Eveson, *Justification by Faith Alone* (Leominster, UK: Day One Publications, 1996), 193.

5 John MacArthur, *2 Timothy: MacArthur New Testament Commentary* (Chicago, IL: Moody Press, 1995), 200; "in this context it seems more appropriate to take righteousness as an appositive, describing the crown."

similar to the glorification of believers (which it seems is what that crown is referring to). This glory is what Paul is referring to in Romans 8:18, "For I consider that the sufferings of this present time are not worthy to be compared with the glory that is to be revealed to us." That "glory" is the glory of Christ (2 Cor. 4:4, 6; Heb. 1:3), into which believers will be transformed (2 Cor. 3:18; Rom. 8:17).

The crown of life is mentioned in Revelation 2:10, "Be faithful until death, and I will give you the crown of life." Here the risen and glorified Christ acknowledges that the church at Smyrna (2:8) will face severe persecution: "Do not fear what you are about to suffer. Behold, the devil is about to cast some of you into prison, so that you will be tested, and you will have tribulation for ten days" (2:10). But the promise is that even if this persecution results in death, they will have the "crown of life." Some think this is a crown only for martyrs, but it is better to see this as the life which all believers will enjoy with Christ. James also wrote about this crown: "Blessed is a man who perseveres under trial; for once he has been approved, he will receive the crown of life which the Lord has promised to those who love Him" (James 1:12). Here James makes clear that the crown of life is for all who love Him (that is, believe in and obey Him [John 15:10; 1 John 5:3]).

This is the life Jesus spoke of: "I came that they may have life, and have it abundantly" (John 10:10), and of which the apostle John wrote: "This is the promise which He Himself made to us: eternal life" (1 John 2:25).

To summarize, in the end, these crowns are not so much additional benefits or added advantages to the salvation or eternal life that all believers will enjoy; they are the culmination of that salvation and the full experience of that eternal life that awaits them in heaven.

Why believers should long for Heaven

Many believers, particularly in prosperous Western countries do not long for heaven; indeed, they do not think much about heaven at all until they are confronted with death. But they should.

- First, because their heavenly Father is there (Matt. 6:9), and their Lord and Savior is there (Heb. 7:25; 9:24).
- Second, because their departed loved ones are there (2 Cor. 5:8) and will come with Him from there (1 Thess. 4:14).
- Third, because their names are there (Luke 10:20).

- Fourth, because their inheritance is there (1 Pet. 1:4).
- Fifth, because their citizenship is there (Phil. 3:20).
- Sixth, because their eternal reward is there (Matt. 5:12).
- Seventh, because their eternal home his there (John 14:3).

Study Questions:

1. What are the several meanings of heaven?
2. What are the biblical reasons believers think "heaven is where God is"?
3. What does "paradise" mean?
4. What does "glorification" mean?
5. Will believers be reunited in heaven with loved ones in Christ?
6. What are the aspects of life in heaven believers hope for?
7. What will not be in heaven?
8. What are the rewards believers can expect in heaven?

Conclusion

My mother passed into the presence of the Lord in May of 2020, not from COVID-19 but during COVID-19. I was with her when she went into hospice and I spent over a month in her apartment just down the hall from her hospice care room. She was too weak and frail to have any more of our conversations about life and death, and heaven, but I would read the Bible with her, and pray with her, and answer the questions she had asked me in our previous conversations.

As the COVID-19 crisis worsened I was not able to remain with her and I was not with her when she passed. But the last thing I said to her, as I held her face in my hands, was "I will see you in heaven."

And I know I will. Thank you, Jesus.

APPENDIX A

THE ONLY ASSURED MEANS OF ARRIVING IN HEAVEN

AS NOTED IN THE Introduction, this small book is about personal eschatology, which concerns the personal destiny of all human beings after death. Throughout this book the lines have been starkly drawn between the destiny of the believer and that of the unbeliever. These terms—believer and unbeliever—have been chosen and used throughout this book deliberately to indicate the basic reason for the contrast between those who will arrive in heaven and those who, sadly and woefully, will enter the eternal darkness and punishment of hell. Those destinies turn on whether one believes or not.

A believer has *faith in* (knows, trusts, and commits himself or herself to) Jesus Christ as Savior and Lord. A believer does not trust in his or her good works, or in religious rites, or religious heritage. A believer does not expect to reach heaven due to his or her personal morality. A believer trusts in the shed blood of Jesus Christ alone, as expressed by the Reformation slogan *Solus Christus*.[1] A believer looks to the cross of Jesus Christ—His sacrificial, substitutionary death—as the only sufficient payment for his or her sins. An unbeliever rejects or denies—or simply does not know or trust in—Jesus Christ and His death on the cross for sinners. This appendix is a brief summary of the truths one must believe about Jesus.

First Truth: The first truth one must embrace to be a believer is the fact that all men are unrighteous sinners before God. The apostle Paul states this

1 The five *solas* of the Reformation, which distinguished the teaching of the Reformers from that of the Roman Catholic Church, are *sola scriptura* (Scripture alone), *solus Christus* (Christ alone), *sola fide* (faith alone), *sola gratia* (grace alone), and *soli Deo gloria* (glory to God alone). These slogans mainly pertain to the doctrine of salvation. The teaching of the Bible alone (*sola*) reveals the essential truths of salvation; Christ's sacrificial death is the only ground of forgiveness of sin and salvation; faith alone is the only means of receiving salvation; grace alone is the only basis for salvation; and the glory of God alone is the final reason for salvation.

clearly in Romans 3:23: "for all have sinned and fall short of the glory of God." Earlier in that same chapter he puts that same truth in these words: "there is none righteous, no not one" (3:9). In fact, it is even worse than that, for the truth is all men are "totally depraved"—which means they are not just prone to sin, but they are sinners from the heart, as the prophet Jeremiah puts it: "The heart is more deceitful than all else, / And is desperately sick" (Jer. 17:9).

Second Truth: As noted in this book, the fact that all are sinners means that all are subject to death. The prophet Ezekiel affirms this: "The soul [person] who sins will die" (18:4). The penalty for sin is death. As Paul says in Romans 6:23, "the wages of sin is death."

Third Truth: The Scriptures make it very clear that we can do nothing to pay that penalty or atone for our sin to prevent the death we must pay. We cannot earn our deliverance from death by good works, or by keeping the Law of God—as Paul says in Romans 3:20, "by the works of the Law no flesh will be justified in His sight." In Ephesians 2:8–9 Paul writes, "For by grace you have been saved through faith; and that not of yourselves, it is the gift of God; not as a result of works, so that no one may boast."

Fourth Truth: God will not accept anyone into heaven without 100-percent, perfect righteousness: "the unrighteous will not inherit the kingdom of God" (1 Cor. 6:9). However, as noted previously, "THERE IS NONE RIGHTEOUS, NOT EVEN ONE" (Rom. 3:10). This puts all mankind, every single human being, in a hopeless situation.

Fifth Truth: But God has provided the solution to this situation. This is the gospel, or "good news" of Jesus Christ. Paul writes of this "good news" in Romans 1:16–17: "For I am not ashamed of the gospel, for it is the power of God for salvation to everyone who believes, to the Jew first and also to the Greek. For in it the righteousness of God is revealed from faith to faith; as it is written, 'But the righteous man shall live by faith.'"

What Paul is saying here is that, when one puts his or her faith in, believes in, Jesus Christ, then God credits, or reckons, or counts the righteousness of Christ to the one who believes in Christ. This is called the imputation of Christ's righteousness to the repentant one who believes. Paul writes in Second Corinthians 5:21, "He made Him who knew no sin to be sin on our behalf, so that we might become the righteousness of God in Him." When one has put all of his or her faith in Christ alone to pay for the penalty for his or her sins, then the righteousness of Christ's sinless life and the payment for sins accomplished by His death is credited to that person's account before God. Then that one—who is now a believer—is saved (Eph. 2:8–9) and has the assurance of arriving in heaven.

Sixth Truth: Jesus Christ came into the world to live a righteous life, and to die on the cross as a sacrifice for sin. This is the message of the "gospel," the "good news." God sent His Son (John 3:16) to live the perfect life—to obey the commands of the law that His people broke—and to shed His blood to cover the guilt of their sin (Col. 2:9; 2 Cor. 5:21; Rom. 5:8). He rose from the grave, ascended to heaven, and now sits at the right hand of the Father (Rom. 4:25; 1 Cor. 15:4; John 20:17; Acts 1:9; Rom. 8:34). "He who has the Son has the life; he who does not have the Son of God does not have the life" (1 John 5:12). Only those who trust in Jesus' sacrifice alone as the payment for their sins will go to heaven. Anyone who rejects Christ or fails to trust in Him alone will not go to heaven. "Whoever believes in him is not condemned, but whoever does not believe stands condemned already because they have not believed in the name of God's one and only Son" (John 3:18, NIV).

Seventh Truth: The Holy Spirit uses the truth of the gospel preached to cause men and women to be "born again" (John 3:5–8; 1 Pet. 1:3; Titus 3:5; Rom. 10:9–10) to eternal life. That Spirit seals (Eph. 1:13) and sanctifies (1 Pet. 1:2; 2 Thess. 2:13) the believer so that he or she may walk by (live by) the Spirit (Gal. 5:16–17), which results in good works (Eph. 2:10; Gal. 5:22–23) and moral living (Rom. 13:13; Gal. 5:24).

Appendix B
A Dispensational, Premillennial Overview of End-Time Events

THIS BOOK IS WRITTEN from a premillennial, dispensational view of eschatology. That view begins with some key presuppositions and affirms several distinctive doctrinal positions. Based on these presuppositions and doctrinal positions, premillennial dispensationalism recognizes that God has revealed in the Bible a divine plan that lays out a clear program of end-time events, such as a future for ethnic national Israel that fulfills the Old Testament covenant promises to that nation (see Gen. 12:1–3; 15; 2 Sam. 7; Jer. 31). This appendix will briefly identify the most important presuppositions and doctrinal positions and briefly summarize that program of end-time events.

Presuppositions

The Bible must be interpreted by using a grammatical, historical (literal) hermeneutic (i.e., a method of interpretation). "A literal method seeks to understand the words of the passage in their normal, natural, and customary meaning within the context. This method searches for the intended meaning of the Biblical author."[1]

This method of interpretation leads to the realization that the nation of Israel in the Bible and the church in the New Testament are distinct "peoples of God." That is, while each may be called "the people of God" in some sense, they are not "the people of God" in the same sense.

The nation of Israel is a "people of God" ethnically descended from Abraham, with national promises from God that pertain to them exclusively as national-ethnic people. Principal among these promises is a "land" (Gen. 12:1; 15:18; 17:8), a king (Gen. 17:6, 16; 36:31; 2 Sam. 7:12, 16) and an earthly kingdom with the city of Jerusalem as its capital city.

1 Alan D. Cole, "The Grammatical-Historical Hermeneutic," *Faith Pulpit*, October 2020 (Ankeny, IA: Faith Theological Seminary), 1.

The fulfillment of these promises of land, king, and kingdom will take place literally, in history, in time, on earth, in the literal land in which Abraham lived, and in the very city where David set his throne—namely Jerusalem. At that time the nation of Israel will be regathered (Isa. 11:11–12; Jer. 32:37; Ezek. 36:24; Zeph. 3:20) and Jesus Christ will return to set up His kingdom and establish His throne (Rev. 19–20; Matt. 24:29–31).

These promises to the nation also included promises of salvation and forgiveness of sin, based on a provision God Himself would provide through a "Suffering Servant" (Isa. 53), also known as the Messiah; these promises (salvation and forgiveness) are a major part of the New Covenant promises as recorded in Jeremiah 31:31–40 (see also Ezek. 36:25–27).

The church, on the other hand, is a "people of God" (or more specifically the body of Christ) that is neither national nor ethnic but is made up of Jews and Gentiles (Rom. 10:12; Gal. 3:28)—indeed, made up of believers from "every tribe and tongue and people and nation" (Rev. 5:9). The church does not supersede or replace the nation of Israel so as to assume the promises God made to Israel, because "the gifts and promises of God" to Israel "are irrevocable" (Rom. 11:29). The church does (that is, individual members of the body of Christ do) participate in the promises of salvation—they do so by faith in the Savior (3:21–30), who is the self-same "Suffering Servant" promised to Israel, who is One and the same Jesus Christ—the Messiah and the Savior of the world (John 3:16).

Overview of End-time Events

Many Old Testament prophecies of a Savior-Messiah were fulfilled at the first coming of Jesus of Nazareth (Matt. 1:21; Luke 1:68–69, 77; 2:30–32). These prophecies were fulfilled literally—such as the place of His birth (Matt. 2:5–6; Mic. 5:2); the ministry of His forerunner (Matt. 3:3; Isa. 40:3); and the events of His death (Matt. 27:35; Ps. 22:18). The expectation is that the prophecies of His second coming will be fulfilled in the same manner—literally.

The next event on the prophetic timetable is the rapture of the church (1 Thess. 4:13–18; 1 Cor. 15:50–53). This will be the fulfillment of the promise Jesus made to His disciples:

> Do not let your heart be troubled; believe in God, believe also in Me. In My Father's house are many dwelling places; if it were not so, I would have told you; for I go to prepare a place for you. If I go and prepare a place for you, I will come again and receive you to Myself, that where I am, there you may be also. (John 14:1–3)

This is the event Paul described in First Thessalonians 4:13–18 (see Chapter 10, on the rapture).

At this time, while the tribulation is happening on earth (see later in this appendix), the church will experience the so-called "*bema* seat" judgment, which Paul describes to the Romans: "For we will all stand before the judgment seat of God. . . . So then each one of us will give an account of himself to God" (Rom. 14:10, 12). He echoes this teaching to the Corinthians: "For we must all appear before the judgment seat of Christ, so that each one may be recompensed for his deeds in the body, according to what he has done, whether good or bad" (2 Cor. 5:10). These passages refer to believers (Christians), not unbelievers, and this judgment is not about salvation, nor is it for the purpose of punishment, but is about rewards (gained or lost). Also, after this the church will enjoy the marriage supper of the Lamb (Rev. 19:9).

After the church has been "caught up," the next event will be the seventieth week of Daniel (Dan. 9:24–27), also called the period of the tribulation (Matt. 24:21, 29). This is the last "week" (seven-year period) of the time for the nation and the city (i.e., the Jewish people and Jerusalem) that the angel Gabriel revealed to Daniel (Dan. 9:21–27). "Seventy weeks have been decreed for your people and your holy city" (9:24). The majority of those weeks (483 years) ended when the Messiah came and was "cut off" (9:26). One week remains and that week is what Jesus describes in Matthew 24 and the apostle John describes in Revelation 4–9. Many Old Testament prophetic books describe this time as well. At the end of the tribulation, the Old Testament saints (Dan. 12:2) and tribulation martyrs (Rev. 20:4) will be raised to enter the Kingdom.

At this point the Lord Jesus Himself, having returned (Matt. 24:29–31; Rev. 19:11–16), will establish His kingdom (Isa. 2:2–4; 9:6–7; 11:1–16; Dan. 2:44; Amos 9:11–15; Mic. 4:1–8). This kingdom will last a thousand years (Rev. 20:2–7). The Latin word for "thousand" is *milia* and so this is called the millennial kingdom or simply the millennium.

After the thousand years of the millennium, there will be the great white throne judgment (Rev. 20:11). Here all the rest of the dead, that is all those who were neither the church-age saints, nor the Old Testament saints, nor the tribulation martyrs, will be judged. They will be judged on the basis of their deeds (20:13), and if their names are not found "written in the book of life" they will be "thrown into the lake of fire" (20:15).

The final phase of the end-times program of God is appearance of "a new heaven and a new earth" (21:1), the most striking feature of which will be the New Jerusalem (21:10).

CLC PUBLICATIONS

Fort Washington, PA 19034

This book is published by CLC Publications, an outreach of CLC Ministries International. The purpose of CLC is to make evangelical Christian literature available to all nations so that people may come to faith and maturity in the Lord Jesus Christ. We hope this book has been life changing and has enriched your walk with God through the work of the Holy Spirit. If you would like to know more about CLC, we invite you to visit our website:

www.clcusa.org

To learn more about the remarkable story of the founding of CLC International, we encourage you to read

LEAP OF FAITH

Norman Grubb
Paperback
Size 5 1/4 x 8, Pages 248
ISBN: 978-0-87508-650-7
ISBN (*e-book*): 978-1-61958-055-8